Japan's Re-emergence as a 'Normal' Military Power

Christopher W. Hughes

ADELPHI PAPER 368-9

9530174

Oxford University Press, Great Clarendon Street, Oxford OX2 6DP
Oxford New York

Athens Auckland Bangkok Bombay Calcutta Cape Town
Dar es Salaam Delhi Florence Hong Kong Istanbul Karachi
Kuala Lumpur Madras Madrid Melbourne Mexico City Nairobi
Paris Taipei Tokyo Toronto
and associated companies in Ibadan

Oxford is a trade mark of Oxford University Press

Published in the United States
by Oxford University Press Inc., New York

© The International Institute for Strategic Studies 2004

First published November 2004 by **Oxford University Press** for
The International Institute for Strategic Studies
Arundel House, 13–15 Arundel Street, Temple Place, London WC2R 3DX
www.iiss.org

Director John Chipman
Editor Tim Huxley
Copy Editor Jill Dobson
Production Simon Nevitt

British Library Cataloguing in Publication Data
Data available

Library of Congress Cataloguing in Publication Data

ISBN 0-19-856758-8
ISSN 0567-932X

Contents

Glossary

ACSA	Acquisition and Cross Servicing Agreement
APEC	Asia-Pacific Economic Cooperation
APT	ASEAN Plus Three
ARF	ASEAN Regional Forum
ASDF	Air Self Defence Force
ASEAN	Association of Southeast Asian Nations
ASEAN-ISIS	ASEAN-Institutes of Strategic and International Studies
ASW	anti-submarine warfare
AWACS	Airborne Warning and Control System
AWS	Aegis war-fighting system
ATSML	Anti-Terrorism Special Measures Law
BADGE	Base Air Defence Ground Environment
BMC4I	Battle Management Command, Control, Computers and Intelligence
BMD	Ballistic Missile Defence
BPI	boost phase intercept
BPND	Basic Policy for National Defence
BSBMD	Bilateral Study on Ballistic Missile Defence
CCS	Central Command and Control System
CIA	Central Intelligence Agency
CIRO	Cabinet Information Research Office
CLB	Cabinet Legislation Bureau
COE	Common Operating Environment
CSCAP	Council for Security Cooperation in the Asia Pacific
CSIC	Cabinet Satellite Intelligence Centre
DD	Destroyer
DDH	Destroyer-Helicopter
DE	Destroyer-Escort
DIC	Defence Intelligence Committee
DII	Defence Information Infrastructure
DPJ	Democratic Party of Japan
DPSS	Defence Policy Studies Subcommittee
DSP	Defence Support Programme
EEZ	Exclusive Economic Zone

FS-X	Fighter Support Experimental
G-NET	Ground Self Defence Force Network
GPR	Global Posture Review
GSDF	Ground Self Defence Force
HNS	Host Nation Support
ICBM	Intercontinental Ballistic Missile
IIPS	Institute for International Policy Studies
IPCL	International Peace Cooperation Law
IRST	infrared search and tracking
LCSMHRA	Law Concerning Special Measures on Humanitarian and Reconstruction Assistance
JCG	Japan Coast Guard
JDA	Japan Defence Agency
JDAM	Joint Direct Attack Munition
JDIH	Japan Defence Intelligence Headquarters
JIIA	Japan Institute of International Affairs
JSC	Joint Staff Council
JSDF	Japan Self Defence Forces
JSO	Joint Staff Organisation
KEDO	Korean Peninsula Energy Development Organisation
MBT	main battle tank
METI	Ministry of Economy, Trade and Industry
MIRV	multiple independently targetable re-entry vehicles
MOF	Ministry of Finance
MOF	Maritime Operational Fleet
MOFA	Ministry of Foreign Affairs
MOX	mixed oxide fuel
MPD	Metropolitan Police Department
MSA	Mutual Security Assistance
MSDF	Maritime Self Defence Force
MTDP	Mid-Term Defence Programme
NATO	North Atlantic Treaty Organisation
NDPO	National Defence Programme Outline
NEACD	Northeast Asia Cooperation Dialogue
NIDS	National Institute of Defence Studies
NIRA	National Institute for Research Advancement
NPA	National Police Agency
NPR	National Police Reserve
NPT	Non-Proliferation Treaty

NSC	National Security Council [of Japan]
NSF	National Safety Force
NTWD	Navy Theatre Wide Defence
ODA	Official Development Assistance
OPK	ocean peacekeeping
PAC-2	*Patriot* Advanced Capability-2
PAC-3	*Patriot* Advanced Capability-3
PAMS	Pacific Armies Management Seminar
PARC	Policy Affairs Research Council
PGM	precision guided munitions
PKO	peacekeeping operation
POL	petroleum, oil, and lubricants
PSI	Proliferation Security Initiative
PSIA	Public Security Investigation Agency
RIMPAC	Rim of the Pacific
RIPS	Research Institute for Peace and Security
RMA	Revolution in Military Affairs
SACO	Special Action Committee on Facilities and Areas in Okinawa
SAM	surface-to-air missile
SAR	synthetic aperture radar
SBIRS	Space Based Infrared System
SCC	Security Consultative Committee
SDC	Subcommittee for Defence Cooperation
SDI	Strategic Defence Initiative
SDIO	Strategic Defence Initiative Office
SDPJ	Social Democratic Party of Japan
SEATO	Southeast Asia Treaty Organisation
SIGINT	Signals Intelligence
SLOC	Sea Lanes of Communication
SMD	Sea-Based Midcourse System
SOFA	Status of Forces Agreement
TCOG	Trilateral Coordination and Oversight Group
TDS	Terminal Defence Segment
TMDWG	Theatre Missile Defence Working Group
TRDI	Technology Research and Development Institute
TSD	Trilateral Security Dialogue
UAV	Unmanned Aerial Vehicles
UN	United Nations

UNTAC	UN Transitional Authority Cambodia
VSTOL	vertical/short takeoff and landing
WPNS	Western Pacific Naval Symposium
WESTPAC	Western Pacific Missile Architecture
WMD	weapons of mass destruction

Tables and Charts

Introduction

Is Japan re-emerging as a great military power, or rather, as some would argue, a 'normal' military power in regional and global security affairs? Or is Japan likely to stay its post-war course of maintaining highly circumscribed military responsibilities outside its own territory and exploring non-military approaches to security? Japan's enhanced security activity over the last decade, especially its unprecedented response to the attacks of 11 September and the US-led 'war on terror', certainly provides grounds for considering whether and how far Japan is seeking to abandon many of the self-imposed constraints on its exercise of military power; how far it is finally functioning as a more reliable US ally; and how far it is once again becoming an assertive military actor in East Asia and beyond. The purpose of this *Adelphi Paper* is to assess these recent developments and to determine their significance for the overall trajectory of Japan's security policy and, in turn, the impact of a changing Japanese security posture on the stability of the East Asia region.

In particular, this paper addresses a subset of questions on the overall trajectory and significance of Japan's potentially 'normal' security policy. It focuses on the current drivers of Japan's security policy, in terms of the international security environment and domestic policy-making system, that are capable of generating change and emergence as a 'normal' military actor. The paper further examines how developments in the three key components of Japan's security policy over the past decade – namely, its individual national defence doctrines and military capabilities; the US–Japan bilateral alliance; and multilateralism (in the form of regional security dialogue, the United Nations and multinational coalitions) – have affected its choice of frameworks through which to channel its military power. Finally, the paper concludes by asking if these developments mean that Japan, as is often speculated, is becoming a more independent military actor, or a more committed US ally, or is establishing a new multilateral role, and what sort of impact these developments will have on international security.

Is Japan's security policy moving in radical directions?

Following 11 September, the Japanese government under Prime Minister Junichiro Koizumi acted swiftly, passing an Anti-Terrorism Special Measures Law (ATSML) in the National Diet on 29 October. The ATSML has enabled, from November 2001 onwards, the dispatch of Japan Self Defence Forces (JSDF) units to the Indian Ocean area to provide logistical support to US and multinational coalition forces engaged in Afghanistan. On 26 July 2003, the Diet passed a Law Concerning Special Measures on Humanitarian and Reconstruction Assistance (LCSMHRA), which has enabled JSDF deployment to provide logistical support for US and coalition forces in Iraq. At the same time that the Japanese government has pursued initiatives to assist US-led campaigns against terrorism and the proliferation of weapons of mass destruction (WMD) in the Middle East, the resurgence of concerns about North Korea's nuclear programme since 2002, after the first crisis of 1993–94, has added momentum to the strengthening of Japan's security posture in East Asia. Between June 2003 and June 2004, the Diet passed, by large majorities, a total of ten related national emergency bills that establish, for the first time in the post-war period, a comprehensive framework to strengthen Japanese government and JSDF domestic authority to respond to a direct attack upon Japan. Japan's new military assertiveness has been shown by the Japan Coast Guard's (JCG) sinking of one of North Korea's 'spy ships' in the East China Sea in December 2001; intimations from government officials that they are prepared to consider long-range air strikes against North Korea's ballistic missile sites if it were to repeat its August 1998 *Taepo-dong-1* launch over Japan; and the government's commitment in December 2003 to procure a Ballistic Missile Defence (BMD) system. This second North Korean nuclear crisis (sparked in 2002–03 by accusations that the North was continuing the clandestine development of nuclear weapons, in spite of its pledge following on from the first nuclear crisis of 1993–94 and under the 1994 Agreed Framework to freeze and eventually dismantle its nuclear programme) has also served to rekindle debate among certain policymakers about the acquisition of Japan's own nuclear deterrent.

Japan's response to instability in the Middle East and Korean Peninsula has been reinforced by its exploration of other areas of military security policy in the post-Cold War period and post-11 September world. The first North Korean nuclear crisis demonstrated the US–Japan alliance's fundamental lack of political and military operability to respond to regional contingencies. This created momentum for the strengthening of the bilateral alliance through the revision of the Guidelines for Japan–US Defence Cooperation from September 1997 onwards, and then the passage through the Diet in May 1999 of legislation (known in Japan as the 'Shuhen Jitaiho') to enable the JSDF to provide logistical support to US forces to defend Japan in the event of regional contingencies around its periphery ('shuhen'). Japan has also developed, under the auspices of the US alliance network in East Asia and independently, new bilateral military exchanges with Australia, South Korea and individual states of the Association of Southeast Asian Nations (ASEAN). In line with these exchanges, Japanese naval power is set to acquire potential new roles in the interdiction of WMD through the Proliferation Security Initiative (PSI) and anti-piracy patrolling across the East Asia region. Japan has demonstrated a new interest in engaging in multilateral security dialogue via the ASEAN Regional Forum (ARF), and in the IISS-hosted Shangri-La Dialogue since 2002.

In the meantime, Japan has bolstered its contribution to United Nations (UN) Peacekeeping Operations (PKO). As a result of its perceived dithering and failure to respond to US and international demands for a 'human contribution' during the 1990–91 Gulf War, Japan eventually dispatched minesweepers to the Gulf after the cessation of hostilities and then passed an International Peace Cooperation Law (IPCL) in June 1992 to allow for JSDF dispatch on limited UN PKO missions, the first of these being in Cambodia in 1992–93. In December 2001, Japan further relaxed restrictions on JSDF participation in 'core' PKO activities, and dispatched its largest-ever contingent of 680 Ground Self Defence Force (GSDF) troops to assist in non-combat reconstruction activities in East Timor from February

Expansion of the JSDF geographical range of dispatch

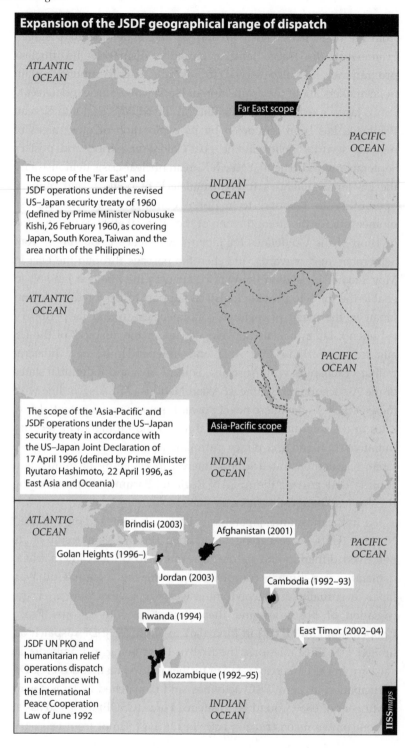

ATLANTIC OCEAN

Far East scope

PACIFIC OCEAN

INDIAN OCEAN

The scope of the 'Far East' and JSDF operations under the revised US–Japan security treaty of 1960 (defined by Prime Minister Nobusuke Kishi, 26 February 1960, as covering Japan, South Korea, Taiwan and the area north of the Philippines.)

ATLANTIC OCEAN

PACIFIC OCEAN

The scope of the 'Asia-Pacific' and JSDF operations under the US–Japan security treaty in accordance with the US–Japan Joint Declaration of 17 April 1996 (defined by Prime Minister Ryutaro Hashimoto, 22 April 1996, as East Asia and Oceania)

Asia-Pacific scope

INDIAN OCEAN

ATLANTIC OCEAN

Brindisi (2003)

Afghanistan (2001)

PACIFIC OCEAN

Golan Heights (1996–)

Jordan (2003)

Cambodia (1992–93)

Rwanda (1994)

East Timor (2002–04)

JSDF UN PKO and humanitarian relief operations dispatch in accordance with the International Peace Cooperation Law of June 1992

Mozambique (1992–95)

INDIAN OCEAN

IISSmaps

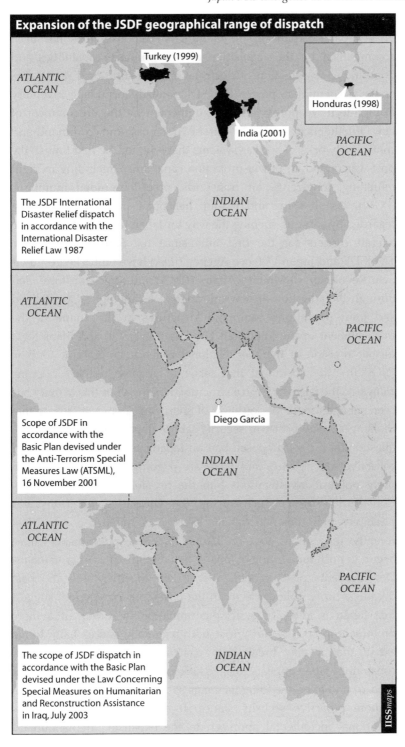

Expansion of the JSDF geographical range of dispatch

Turkey (1999)

ATLANTIC
OCEAN

Honduras (1998)

India (2001)

PACIFIC
OCEAN

INDIAN
OCEAN

The JSDF International
Disaster Relief dispatch
in accordance with the
International Disaster
Relief Law 1987

ATLANTIC
OCEAN

PACIFIC
OCEAN

Diego Garcia

Scope of JSDF in
accordance with the
Basic Plan devised under
the Anti-Terrorism Special
Measures Law (ATSML),
16 November 2001

INDIAN
OCEAN

ATLANTIC
OCEAN

PACIFIC
OCEAN

The scope of JSDF dispatch in
accordance with the Basic Plan
devised under the Law Concerning
Special Measures on Humanitarian
and Reconstruction Assistance
in Iraq, July 2003

INDIAN
OCEAN

IISS*maps*

2002 onwards.

Japan's expansion of its military responsibilities has been accompanied by the acquisition of new military capabilities and domestic re-examination of doctrinal and constitutional restrictions on the use of military power. The JSDF's already formidable inventory of high-tech weaponry is being augmented by the procurement of new intelligence satellites, missile defences and command-and control-networks; as well as systems that hint, for the first time in the post-war period, at power-projection capabilities, including in-flight refuelling, long-range air transports, precision-guided munitions (PGM), assault ships and flat-top helicopter transports – the last regarded by some as opening the way for Japan to once again acquire aircraft carriers for the first time since the Second World War. The JSDF and Japan Defence Agency (JDA) have embarked on their own Revolution in Military Affairs (RMA) and force transformation through the adoption of new information technologies, streamlined and joint operations command structures in the shape of the establishment of the Joint Staff Organisation (JSO), and plans for a further revision of the 1995 National Defence Programme Outline (NDPO) – the document that sets out Japanese military doctrine alongside the necessary force structure. Finally, all of this activity has been set against the background of sharpened domestic debate that challenges many post-war security taboos. Japan's policymakers are questioning the self-imposed ban on Japan's exercise of the right of collective self defence, and there are ongoing Diet committee and party political investigations into the revision of Article 9 of the Constitution from which spring the various prohibitions and principles that constrain Japan's exercise of military power. Most recently, throughout 2004, influential Japanese policymakers have begun to push for a lifting of Japan's ban on the export of armaments. Developments post-11 September, taken together with the past decade security policy activity in the post-Cold War period, suggest that Japan is intensifying its determination to carve out a more prominent military security role, both regionally and globally, to the extent that it may break with past domestic and international constraints. Japan appears to have kicked the 'Gulf War syndrome' of 1990–91 and to be shedding its image as a 'reactive state' in favour of a more proactive security stance. It appears less reliant on its traditional incremental approach to the expansion of its military security role. Japan has shown an uncharacteristic speed and appetite for passing successive rounds of new security legislation. The ATSML required less than three weeks of relatively unimpeded policy deliberation and 33 hours of Diet debate, compared to the tempestuous Diet debates on the IPCL, which took nine months, and the tortuous definitional debates on the geographical and functional scope of the Jitaiho Shuhen , which took close to one year.

Japan's recent security activity embodies also greater geographical and functional substance. Recent JSDF missions in the Indian Ocean represent its first official overseas dispatch during an ongoing conflict, and the JSDF has gained a new mandate to use weapons for the protection of not only its own units but also the military personnel of the US and other states and refugees. Japan appears to be losing its usual reticence about providing active support for its US ally and is learning how to interact militarily in multilateral 'coalitions of the willing'. The speculation has even been that Japan could function as the 'Great Britain of the Far East' – performing the role of a loyal East Asian ally prepared to back US efforts to face down the remaining elements of the 'axis of evil'.

Why Japan matters for international security

Japan's potential re-emergence as a 'normal' military power has vital implications for East Asian and global security. Much security analysis of East Asia in recent years has been fixated on the economic and military rise of China and the consequences for regional stability. By contrast, recession-hit Japan has moved out of the media and academic spotlight, with the concomitant result that important developments in its security policy have undergone less consistent scrutiny. This collective myopia towards Japan as a security actor is unwise: in the immediate future, it is more likely to be Japan's resurgence as a significant military actor, undergirded by massive technological and economic resources, and the possession of genuine regional-wide power-projection capabilities, which will determine the balance of power in East Asia.

Japan's choices about the frameworks within which it deploys its expanded military power will be decisive for regional stability and, indeed, for the international order as a whole. Japan's future willingness to channel its military capabilities bilaterally via the framework of a strengthened US–Japan alliance will be crucial for the

US in terms of its ability to mobilise regional allies in support of its military hegemonic status in East Asia and globally. In turn, this willingness will be a pivotal factor in determining the outcome of US policy in dealing with North Korea and China. Japanese preparedness to explore new or expanded multilateral military security options will determine, in large part, the course of East Asian security cooperation and will affect the functioning of UN PKO and other security activities. Moreover, if Japan were to show reluctance to harness its military power either through the framework of the bilateral alliance or through East Asian or UN-centred multi-lateralism, and were to strike out instead in a more independent direction, then the future security scenario in East Asia would be highly uncertain. Just as importantly, Japan's potential predilection for an augmented military security role will have wider ramifications for alternative approaches to security in a post-Cold War world. This is because, as already indicated, Japan's devotion of policy energy and material resources to military security may carry a heavy opportunity cost with regard to its ability to pursue simultaneous non-military and economic approaches to security. If Japan, as a major economic power and traditional standard-bearer for alternative security policies, is seen to falter in this regard, then it may also throw into doubt its support for non-military approaches to security, and consequently, the ability of other states and international organisations to pursue them without Japan's involvement.

Structure and arguments

Japan's record of military activity over the past decade and since 11 September, combined with its intrinsic importance as a regional and now global military actor, and the sense that Japan is poised on the brink of major decisions about its military status, make a detailed analysis of Japan's security policy vital at this juncture. As stated above, the objective of this *Adelphi Paper* (the first in more than ten years to exclusively address the issue of Japan, and coinciding with the fiftieth anniversary of the establishment of the JSDF, and release of a revised NDPO) is to take stock of recent developments and to investigate in depth exactly what they mean for the future trajectory of Japan's security policy, and its repercussions for East Asian security and beyond. The paper addresses these overarching questions in a series of chapters that analyse key issues in Japan's developing military posture, and which are then used as components to build a larger explanation of the overall direction of Japanese policy.

Chapter 1 investigates the domestic and international framework that has determined the past course of Japanese security policy in order to contextualise and gauge the significance of recent developments. In particular, it focuses on the evolution of Japan's military role from the post-war baseline of the Yoshida Doctrine. Chapter 2 then considers in what ways the changing international structure surrounding Japan, and especially China and North Korea's military behaviour, and the events of 11 September and the response of the US and UN, are driving Japan's interest in expanding its military role. The chapter also examines Japan's domestic debate on a 'normal' security role, the evolving policy structure, and the shifting influence among key policymakers and their attitudes to the enhanced exercise of military power. It considers whether Japan's security policy initiatives are simply the product of the extraordinary international and domestic circumstances of the post-11 September security environment and Koizumi's premiership, or if they represent the culmination of more fundamental trends making for a sea change in its defence stance. Chapter 3 probes developments in Japan's national military capabilities and how they are affecting the orientation and autonomy of its military policy. Among other issues, the chapter explores Japan's enactment of new legal frameworks and military doctrines, the procurement of new defensive and power projection capabilities, the ongoing reorganisation of the JSDF, and the debate on a Japanese nuclear option. Chapter 4 analyses the strengthening of the Japan–US alliance framework in the post-Cold War period, how far Japan has been willing to integrate its military capabilities with those of its bilateral alliance partner, and the resultant implications for Japan's independence as a military actor and the maintenance of US power in East Asia. The chapter includes coverage of the revised Guidelines for Japan–US Defence Cooperation, BMD, Okinawa and bases issues, US force realignments and Japan's attitude to US-led wars in Afghanistan and Iraq. Chapter 5 examines Japan's experimentation with multilateral security frameworks in East Asia and under UN and US auspices, and the degree to which these could influence the trajectory of Japanese military policy by creating alternative security paths or by reinforcing existing bilateral and national frameworks. Japan's role in the ARF,

UN PKO and multinational 'coalitions of the willing' in Afghanistan and Iraq is subject to scrutiny.

Extrapolating from these chapters the key determinant variables and trends in Japan's security policy, the principal argument of this paper is that Japan is undoubtedly moving along the trajectory of becoming a more assertive or 'normal' military power, and that the post-11 September security environment has greatly accelerated this trend. Japan has set crucial legal and functional precedents for JSDF deployment in Afghanistan and Iraq, which presages an expanded role for Japan's military power in East Asia and in other regions. These trends have been reinforced by the upgrading of the US–Japan alliance over the last decade, and Japan's strengthening of its independent military capabilities. Japan's renewed fears about North Korea's nuclear programme, and longer-term concerns about China's military intentions, are further propelling its security policy along this more muscular military path. If either of these sources of instability were to become clear and immediate threats to Japan, then, combined with the trends that have served to raise Japan's national military profile in recent years, Japan could quickly reveal itself as a fully fledged military great power.

While Japan is poised to undertake new and expanded military responsibilities, it is not likely to channel its military power through greatly different frameworks than at present. Based on current trends, Japan will probably seek to further strengthen the US–Japan bilateral alliance as its main framework for the utilisation of military power. It is unlikely to devote the greatest share of its military energies to East Asian or UN-centred multilateral frameworks, given the expectation that these cannot provide sufficient guarantees for national defence. Japanese fears of sparking regional instability are also likely to rule out its adopting a more independent security stance. Japan will continue (with, arguably, increasing difficulty) to retain multilateralism and an autonomous defence posture as potential security options to hedge against total dependence on the US, but will only opt for these if the US is seen to fail it as a reliable or indomitable ally. In pursuing this path of ever closer security cooperation with the US, Japan will be forced to discard many of the tenets of the Yoshida Doctrine, and may bind itself inextricably into the bilateral alliance framework. The clear implication for regional and global security is that an augmented US–Japan alliance, with Japan a more active and powerful player within it, will only become an ever more formidable presence in determining international stability.

Chapter 1

Japan's post-war security trajectory and policy system

Fundamental changes in Japan's security strategy and policy-making system – in turn precipitated by changes in the international security environment and domestic politics – will ensure that Japan's recent record of military proactivity is unlikely to be a temporary phenomenon, and that Japan will further shift its overall security trajectory away from its traditionally low-profile approach to regional military affairs.

The Yoshida Doctrine

Japan's traditional reticence to engage directly in regional military affairs clearly originates from its experiences of catastrophic defeat in the Pacific War; the atomic bombings of Hiroshima and Nagasaki; the US-dominated Allied Occupation; Japanese demilitarisation; the adoption of Article 9 of the so-called 'peace constitution' of 1947; and lingering suspicions of Japanese militarism among neighbouring East Asian states. The outcome has been a strong strain of anti-militaristic sentiment amongst Japan's policy-making elites and general citizenry, and a genuine ambivalence about the centrality and efficacy of military power in ensuring security. Japanese caution about the function of military power was reflected in Prime Minister Shigeru Yoshida's formulation of the basic course for Japan's security strategy in the post-war era, later known as the 'Yoshida Doctrine'.

The military path that Yoshida laid down for Japan in the immediate post-war period was alignment – although not necessarily alliance – with the US, coupled with limited national rearmament.

Yoshida did not rule out large-scale rearmament and Japan's re-emergence as a independent military power when the time was ripe, and viewed close US–Japan security cooperation as a temporary expedient.[1] Yoshida realised this policy by seeking and signing the 1951 Security Treaty Between the United States and Japan; the original incarnation of the US–Japan security treaty.

The bilateral security treaty initiated an implicit grand strategic bargain between Japan and the US. Under the treaty, Japan was obliged to provide the US with bases to enable the projection of US military power onto the East Asian continent. In separate agreements, Japan committed itself to assume a degree of responsibility for national self-defence through light rearmament and the formation of the National Police Reserve (NPR) in 1950 and then the National Safety Force (NSF) in 1952 – the forerunners of the JSDF, created in 1954. In return, Japan gained effective (if not explicit, until the revised security treaty of 1960) US guarantees of superpower military protection, including forward-deployed forces in Japan and the extended US nuclear umbrella. In accepting these security arrangements, Japan further gained US assent for the ending of the Occupation, although the US retained administrative control of Okinawa until 1972. Japan's post-war alignment with the US also earned it economic security guarantees in the form of special economic dispensations by the US, such as access to the US market, economic aid and international economic institutions. Thus, through US sponsorship, Japan was able to regain its place in the international community and, furnished as it was with US military protection, was free to pursue its primary post-war goal of economic reconstruction. In addition to meeting the challenges of the post-war international environment, Japan's decision to entrust, in large part, its military security to the US enabled its government to suppress and manage the controversial domestic political issue of Japan's future military role.

Nevertheless, Yoshida was aware that this strategic bargain carried costs as well as benefits for Japan, and that Japan should not commit itself unconditionally. The principal costs of alignment with the US were the classic security dilemmas of abandonment and entrapment. During the formulation of Japan's basic security strategy in the early stages of the Cold War, Yoshida did not fear Japan's abandonment by its US military protector because he perceived that the US valued Japan too highly as a central component of its containment strategy in East Asia. However, for successive Japanese policymakers, the military dependence on the US established by Yoshida, and the knowledge that the US as a global power could have interests that superseded those related to Japan, has engendered the fear that the US's commitment to defend Japan might eventually wane, leaving it highly vulnerable.

The major concern for Yoshida and his successors, though, at the time of the signing of the security treaty and ever since, was the possibility of entrapment in US regional and global military strategy. Japan's provision of bases to the US could make it a proxy target in a nuclear or conventional conflict in the region, or the US might push Japan towards assuming a role beyond its existing function as part of the defensive perimeter for the containment of communism, pressuring it to become a more active player in the Cold War struggle outside its own national territory. Japan's particular fear was that the security arrangement might lead to its entanglement in disastrous conflicts on the Korean Peninsula or over Taiwan.

To minimise the risks of entrapment, Yoshida pursued a number of options to limit Japan's potential military commitments to the US. Under Yoshida's leadership, Japan emphasised that its security policy was predicated upon the principle of individual national self-defence, and rejected any attempt by the US to integrate it into a collective self-defence arrangement. Japan's policymakers were aware that the US, at the time of the negotiation of the security treaty and throughout the early 1950s, wanted to create a regional-wide multilateral collective self-defence network, modelled along the lines of the North Atlantic Treaty Organisation (NATO) and designed to complement the creation of the now defunct Southeast Asia Treaty Organisation (SEATO). Such a network would have obliged Japan to provide military assistance to the US and other US-aligned states in the event of a conflict. Japanese policymakers were also aware of US expectations that, at the very least, Japan might be persuaded to provide bilateral military assistance for the defence of US forces and territory. Japanese awareness of the risks of entrapment and resistance to them were manifested in the final language of the 1951 treaty, in which the 'mutuality' and collective self-defence provisions of bilateral security treaties concluded by the US with other East Asian states in the early Cold War period were notably absent. Moreover, Yoshida further limited the scope of Japanese security commitments to the US by minimising Japan's available military capabilities, frustrating US expectations by steadfastly refusing to develop the type of expeditionary and ground forces that could be used to support US forward deployed forces and US-led coalitions in conflicts in East Asia. Instead, Japan focused upon the gradual build-up of more balanced land, sea and air forces, and indigenous defence production capabilities. These would ensure not only economic recovery, but also that Japan would retain a degree of potential autonomy in security affairs from the US in the future.

Hence, it can be seen that Yoshida's commitment of Japan to the bilateral security treaty with the US did not involve, at this time, any sense of functioning as a true US ally on a par with other treaty partners. Japan was aligned with the US because it was incorporated broadly into the US-led military and capitalist sphere in East Asia, and was the recipient of one-way US security guarantees for its own territory. But Japan did not perceive itself to be strictly allied with the US because it was not prepared to make any kind of active contribution to defend the US, or to support US strategy in the region, and deliberately limited itself to the passive role of the provision of military bases. As will be seen in later sections, Japan's leaders refused to equate the bilateral security treaty with an alliance relationship until the 1980s. Japan's eventual willingness to move from the principle of passive alignment under the Yoshida doctrine to that of an active alliance relationship in later years is, in many ways, the key to understanding the changing trajectory of Japan's military policy.

Cold War adjustments

Japan's basic security strategy trajectory, set by the Yoshida doctrine and underpinned by the strategic bargain with the US, went largely unchanged for much of the early Cold War period, although it underwent a series of adjustments to take account of the fluctuating international security environment and domestic Japanese politics. Prime Ministers Hatoyama Ichiro and Nobusuke Kishi made the first minor adjustments in their negotiations leading up the 1960 revision of the bilateral security treaty. Both sought to remove unequal provisions in the security treaty (relating to the US right to use its forces in Japan to suppress domestic unrest, and the absence of an explicit security guarantee by the US to defend Japan) by offering to inject a greater degree of mutuality into the security treaty.

The negotiations for the revised 1960 Treaty of Mutual Security and Cooperation between the US and Japan set out more clearly, although not unequivocally, the security responsibilities of Japan and the US with regard to each other under the treaty. Article 5 of the treaty provided the first explicit security guarantee by stating that any attack on the territory of Japan was recognised as an attack on both treaty partners. Article 6 pledged that, in order to contribute to its own security, Japan would supply bases to the US for the maintenance of security in the Far East.

Nevertheless, in seeking to revise the treaty, Japan's policymakers continued to pursue options to limit their military commitments to the US and to hedge against entrapment. Japan again made clear, in the course of revision negotiations, that the security treaty was based on the principle of individual national rather than collective self-defence and that Japan would not dispatch troops outside its own territory in support of the US. Japan also succeeded, via Article 4 of the revised treaty and in the exchange of notes that took place afterwards between Prime Minister Kishi and US Secretary of State Christian A. Herter, in negotiating a new US pledge to consult on the implementation of the treaty provisions, on major changes to the deployment of US forces in Japan, and on US combat operations from bases in Japan (apart from those conducted under Article 5 of the treaty). Ever since Japanese policymakers have argued that this provides the Japanese government a final veto over the US introduction of nuclear weapons and the staging of US military operations from Japan. In reality, Japan has turned a blind eye to the passage of nuclear weapons into Japanese ports and has refrained from exercising this veto, for fear of alienating the US. But for Japanese policymakers, the right to refuse cooperation under the security treaty served as one latent means by which to rein in US military operations from Japan if they are seen to impose too great a security cost. Furthermore, Japanese policymakers were able to gain US assent to drop plans for the geographical scope of Article 6 of the treaty to be designated as the 'Asia-Pacific', and to accept the less extensive designation of the 'Far East' as in the original treaty. In Diet interpellations in February 1960, Prime Minister Kishi limited the scope of US–Japan security cooperation by stating that, while the 'Far East' was not necessarily a clearly designated geographical region to which the treaty could be restricted, it broadly included the areas north of the Philippines and surrounding Japan ('Nihon no shuhen'), and the areas under the control of South Korea and Taiwan.

The next moves for the adjustment of Japan's security trajectory and the US–Japan strategic bargain emerged from the US side, spurred by the intensification of Cold War struggles in the 1960s. The US's involvement in the Vietnam War made clear the limitations of its military power and increasingly forced the US to look towards aligned states to shore up its security strategy in East Asia. As the war escalated in the mid-1960s, Prime Ministers Hayato Ikeda and Eisaku Sato were determined that Japan should resist any suggestion that it might follow the US allies South Korea and Australia in dispatching troops to Vietnam to assist the war effort. Instead, Japan's support was limited to the provision of economic aid to South Vietnam and permitting the US to use its bases in Japan to support the war. President Richard Nixon's eventual decision to withdraw from Vietnam and the announcement of the 'Guam Doctrine' of July 1969 signalled the scaling-back of US military commitments in East Asia and enhanced US expectations for treaty partners to undertake responsibility for their own and regional security. This presented further potential US security demands upon Japan. As part of the wider US design to push aligned states towards expanded defence commitments, Japan was obliged to acknowledge, in the Sato–Nixon joint communiqué of November 1969, that South Korea and Taiwan were respectively 'essential' and 'important' factors for Japanese security. Japanese policymakers were fearful of the risks of entrapment involved in drawing this security linkage, but they acquiesced to maintain the US security presence in the region, and as part of the price for the US to agree to the final reversion of Okinawa to Japanese administration in 1972. Moreover, the risks of entrapment were minimised by Japan's ensuring that, in the communiqué and thereafter, it did not provide the US with an explicit pledge to participate directly in a regional security arrangement.

Japan's security strategy and relationship with the US underwent further significant adjustments in the later stages of the Cold War. During the early 1970s, the United States' pursuit of détente with the USSR and rapprochement with China meant that the possibility of Japan being embroiled in a regional conflict was lessened, and created opportunities for Japan to pursue its diplomatic and economic engagement policies vis-à-vis China. Japan's principal fears in this period were, firstly, that bilateral economic frictions, which were becoming more pronounced in the wake of the Japanese economic miracle, would lead to its abandonment by the US as a security partner; and, secondly; the continuing apparent limits of the US to maintain its military hegemony in the region following withdrawal from Vietnam. Japan moved to hedge against abandonment by formulating the NDPO in 1976. The NDPO was the first attempt by Japan to set out the principles of its defence policy alongside the military force structure necessary to achieve them. It was notable in emphasising not only a qualitative build-up of Japan's national military capabilities as an implicit demonstration of efforts to relieve the defensive burdens of the US, but also in its explicit stress that Japan would maintain forces sufficient to defend itself in the first instance from direct aggression, and that if this proved impossible, Japan would seek US support. Thus, Japan was beginning to develop a military doctrine premised upon the closer coordination of Japanese and US forces.

The emergence of the US–Japan 'alliance'

During the late 1970s and 1980s, the enhanced common threat of the USSR forced a convergence of Japanese and US strategic interests. Japan found itself threatened to a more direct and greater degree by the Soviet military build-up in East Asia. As a result, Japanese and US Cold War strategic interests overlapped more clearly, and Japanese policymakers' fears of needless entrapment in a military conflict were lessened. Japan and the US discovered, for the first time, a division of labour for military cooperation under the security treaty. Japan, in line with the principle of individual self-defence, expanded its national military capabilities to assist the US in fulfilling its obligations to defend Japan under Article 5 of the security treaty. This military build-up, although predicated only on the basis of Japan's own individual self-defence, was encouraged by the US, which viewed it as a solid defensive platform from which to project power under Article 6 of the treaty. The GSDF acquired larger numbers of main battle tanks (MBT) and shifted the weight of its deployments to Hokkaido to counter Soviet power in the north. The Air Self Defence Force (ASDF)'s purchase of E-2C early-warning aircraft and F-15 fighters was justified by the need to defend Japanese airspace against Soviet T-26 *Backfire* bombers, but these were also clearly intended, in the event of a conflict, to defend US bases in Japan from Soviet air-strikes and to release US military units from their defensive responsibilities to concentrate on possible combat roles outside Japanese territory. Similarly, the Maritime Self Defence Force (MSDF) procured large numbers of destroyers, minesweepers and P-3C aircraft to assist in Anti-Submarine Warfare (ASW) to provide a defensive shield for the US Navy operating out of Japan.

Japan and the US embarked on the first steps towards the direct coordination of their respective military roles through the formulation of the 1978 Guidelines of Japan–US Defence Cooperation. The Guidelines outlined areas for bilateral cooperation relating to Japan's immediate defence under Article 5 of the security treaty (including tactical planning, joint exercises and logistical support), and for cooperation in regional contingencies in the Far East under Article 6 (including patrolling the Sea Lines of Communication [SLOC]). The fact that Japan's defence efforts were mainly concentrated around Japan itself, and that US military activities, even outside Japanese territory, were clearly seen to contribute to Japan's own security by countering the common Soviet threat, meant that the issue of collective self-defence as a basis for bilateral cooperation was not seriously raised. Subsequently, enhanced bilateral cooperation reinforced Japanese perceptions of the overall utility of the security treaty to the point that, in 1981, Prime Minister Zenko Suzuki was first able to refer publicly to this relationship as an 'alliance'.

Despite the increased willingness of Japanese policymakers to convert the security treaty into a bilateral alliance, they continued to hedge against entrapment in US military strategy. Japan maintained its latent veto on the US use of bases, the limitations on the geographical scope of the security treaty and the predication of its support for the US on the principle of individual national self-defence rather than collective self-defence. Japan's policymakers also ensured that, even though the JSDF's built-up capabilities were increasingly complementary with those of the US, and increasingly skewed to the point that Japan lacked balanced forces to defend itself independently of the US, these capabilities remained fundamentally separate. Japan avoided the integration of the JSDF's command structures with those of the US, fearing that this would erode Japanese control over its own military assets. Japan also carefully avoided joint research in depth with the US into Article 6-type cooperation under the Guidelines, for fear that this could lead to operations outside Japan's own territory. Moreover, Japan continued to seek an indigenous production capacity in key defence technologies, thereby maintaining a degree of security autonomy from the US.

Japan's limited multilateral role

Japan's deepening bilateral alliance cooperation with the US during the Cold War was not matched by any similar impulse for an enhanced Japanese security role via multilateral frameworks. Japan's 1957 Basic Policy for National Defence (BPND) was the first statement of national security policy. The BPND stressed that Japan would support UN activities for international peace, and that Japan would rely on the US–Japan security arrangement only until such time that the UN was capable of functioning to deter aggression. Japan's hopes for achieving a UN-centred security policy that would eventually substitute for the US–Japan security relationship were also incorporated into Articles 6 and 10 of the 1951 and 1960 bilateral security treaties respectively. That Japan valued cooperation within multilateral security frameworks was further indicated by the preamble to both security treaties, which stated that the US–Japan security arrangements were consistent with the UN Charter, and by the preamble of the 1960 security treaty, which further stated that, in accordance with the UN Charter, Japan and the US possessed the rights of individual and collective-self defence.

However, in this period, Japan chose not to pursue a role in multilateral frameworks that would involve a military commitment. It did become an increasingly important supporter, politically and financially, of UN security activities, including PKO, but was not prepared to countenance JSDF dispatch because of constitutional and legal restrictions, explained in more detail below.[2] Japan was unwilling to commit its security strategy to the UN to a greater degree, given concerns that the organisation had been rendered ineffective by Cold War superpower competition, and that it was thus unlikely ever to function as a sufficient security guarantee that could supplement or replace the US–Japan security treaty. An active Japanese military attachment to the UN was thought to conflict with the US bilateral security guarantee, because it would subject Japan to the Cold War tensions within the organisation and detract from its freedom of action to cooperate with the US under the security treaty.

Any potential Japanese commitment to a UN-centred security option was thus subordinated to the exigencies of the US–Japan security arrangement; the principal role of the UN multilateralism espoused in the security treaty was to provide domestic and international legitimacy for bilateral alliance cooperation.

Japan's reluctance to explore UN-centred multilateral security frameworks was paralleled by its reluctance to explore multilateral frameworks at the regional level. Japan's multilateral military security options were largely blocked by its constitutional prohibition from 1954 onwards (explained in more detail in the sections below) that Japan possessed but was unable to exercise the right of collective-self defence. Nevertheless, Japanese policymakers, for a variety of concerns, continued to shy away from plans for multilateral security cooperation in East Asia, whether US-directed or otherwise. The first of these was the concern that any proposed multilateral framework would simply be unable to provide Japan with credible full or even partial security guarantees. Japanese policymakers resisted US plans for the incorporation of Japan into a collective self-defence framework in East Asia because they were unconvinced that it would function effectively, given that many of the partners that the US projected for it had no shared security identity with Japan, and were in fact former adversaries, such as Australia and South Korea, who were strongly disinclined to accept Japan's membership of any type of regional security community. Japan also noted the ultimate failure of the US to mould SEATO into a nascent collective self-defence organisation, given its lack of a genuine multilateral character or political and military coherence. Japanese concerns about the efficacy of multilateral frameworks were also reinforced by fears of entrapment and abandonment. It has already been seen how Japanese policymakers, from the Yoshida era onwards, balked at initial US plans for entering Japan into a collective self-defence relationship that entailed possible overseas JSDF dispatch and entrapment in continental military expeditions. Conversely, Japan feared that proposals for multilateral frameworks in East Asia that did not emanate from the US side during the Cold War could also lead to risks of abandonment. Japan's leaders openly rejected Soviet calls for the establishment of a collective self-defence security system in 1969 and for a regional-wide security community in 1988 for fear that these were attempts to drive a wedge between the US and its bilateral security partners, which would undermine US–Japan security arrangements.

As the Cold War progressed, the Yoshida doctrine underwent various tests and adjustments, but remained essentially intact as the guiding precept for Japan's overall security strategy. The strategic bargain between Japan and the US, and the domestic and international conditions that underlay the Yoshida Doctrine, also remained largely intact, and continued to be seen as reconciling and serving the security interests of both sides. Japan's regional and global military role within these strategic parameters remained limited. Japan did embark upon a quantitative and qualitative build-up of its military capabilities throughout the course of the Cold War, but the JSDF's role was predicated solely upon national individual self-defence and the protection of Japan's own territory. Japan's principal role in regional security was an indirect one, manifested via the bilateral framework of the US–Japan security treaty. Japan's increasing alliance cooperation was crucial in supporting continued US superpower military dominance in East Asia. Nevertheless, the highly asymmetrical nature of the evolving US–Japan alliance meant that Japan's military role was limited. Japan's principle of individual national self-defence meant that it provided for the conventional defence of Japan itself and of US forces based therein in the event of a conflict, but was under no obligation to assist the US outside Japanese territory, and that it remained heavily dependent on US forward deployed forces to deal with any regional crisis that could impact upon its own security. Furthermore, Japan evaded any commitment to multilateral military security frameworks.

Japan's security policy-making system: leaning towards immobilism

Constitutional principles and prohibitions

Japan's adoption of the Yoshida doctrine produced, and was itself the product of, a domestic policy-making system that ensured a consistently low-profile Japanese military stance throughout the Cold War period. As already noted, Japan's predilection for limiting its military security role was in large part derived from wartime defeat and the anti-militaristic principles derived from the 1947 'peace constitution', which ever since have framed the constraints and opportunities of security policymaking in Japan.

The Preamble of the Constitution states Japanese ideals with regard to security:

> *We, the Japanese people, desire peace for all time and are deeply conscious of the high ideals controlling human relationships, and we have determined to preserve our security and existence, trusting in the justice and faith of the peace-loving peoples of the world. We desire to occupy an honoured place in an international society striving for the preservation of peace, and the banishment of tyranny and slavery, oppression and intolerance for all time from the earth. We recognise that all peoples of the world have the right to live in peace, free from fear and want.*

Chapter 2, Article 9 of the Constitution, 'The Renunciation of War', reads as follows:

> *Aspiring sincerely to an international peace based on justice and order, the Japanese people forever renounce war as a sovereign right of the nation and the threat or use of force as means of settling international disputes.*
>
> *In order to accomplish the aim of the preceding paragraph, land, sea, and air forces, as well as other war potential, will never be maintained. The right of belligerency of the state will not be recognised.*

Original drafts of Article 9 drawn up by the Japanese and US sides were intended to prohibit Japan not only from engaging in offensive warfare, but also from using force in national self-defence and from maintaining a military establishment. However, amendments made in the Diet to Article 9 led to the insertion of the phrase 'in order to accomplish the aim of the preceding paragraph', which then opened the way for an interpretation of the Constitution allowing Japan to maintain military forces for other purposes as long as these were not designed as a means of settling international disputes. Japanese governments since the 1950s have interpreted Article 9 as permitting Japan, in line with its position as a sovereign state under the UN Charter, to exercise the right of individual national self-defence ('kobetsuteki jieiken') and to maintain the JSDF for this purpose.

Japan's government, following its interpretation of Article 9, has since pursued an exclusively defence-oriented policy ('senshu boei'), and elaborated a number of other constitutional prohibitions on the exercise of military power. The first of these is that Japan should restrict its military capacity to the minimum necessary for self-defence ('jiei no tame no hitsuyo saisho gendo') and that the JSDF should not possess 'war potential' ('senryoku'). The government argues that the minimum necessary capacity for self-defence and what exactly constitutes 'war potential' are dependent upon the prevailing international situation, military technology levels and the total strength of the JSDF. Hence, this interpretation leaves open the possibility for the JSDF to possess certain types of very powerful weapons, including, as seen below and in Chapter 3, nuclear weapons, if these are deemed to be for the purposes of self-defence. The Japanese government does regard as unconstitutional and prohibits the JSDF from possessing weapons that are viewed as offensive in nature and used exclusively for the destruction of other states, since these exclude the minimum necessary level of self-defence capacities. In practice, this has meant that the JSDF has not possessed power-projection capabilities such as Intercontinental Ballistic Missiles (ICBM), ballistic missiles, long-range strategic bombers, in-flight refuelling aircraft or aircraft carriers.

The second prohibition derived from Article 9 relates to the actual conditions for the exercise of the right of self defence. The Japanese government defines these as an imminent and illegitimate act of aggression against Japan; the absence of an appropriate means to deal with the aggression other than resort to the right of self-defence; and the use of armed force confined to the minimum necessary level. The third prohibition relates to the geographical scope of the exercise of the right of self-defence. The Japanese government stresses that the exercise of the minimum necessary force to defend Japan under the right of self-defence is not necessarily confined to the geographic scope of Japanese territory. Japan has always had the potential under the Constitution to dispatch the JSDF overseas for the purposes of self-defence. However, the government has ruled that overseas JSDF dispatch in most cases would exceed the minimum levels of forces necessary for self-defence. In practice, Japan refrained from JSDF dispatch during the Cold War for fear of entanglement in overseas conflicts, and also because the JSDF Law contained no provision regulating this activity. As a result, until the JSDF Law was amended in June 1992 to allow limited JSDF participation in UN PKO, its overseas dispatch was not necessarily unconstitutional, but definitely illegal.

The fourth prohibition on Japan's use of military force is the constitutional ban on the exercise of the right of collective self-defence ('shudanteki jieiken'). Japan's government recognises that, as a sovereign state, it possesses under Chapter 7 of Article 51 of the UN Charter the inherent right of collective self-defence. Since 1954, though, the Japanese government has taken the position that the actual exercise of this right would exceed the minimum force necessary for the purposes of self-defence and is unconstitutional. Japan does not regard JSDF support for military forces of other states as unconstitutional if these actions do not involve military combat. The range of actions possible has included various forms of logistical support, such as transport, supply, maintenance, medical services, guard duty and communications. During the early stages of the Cold War, as noted above, Japan anticipated demands to change its interpretation of the constitution and to exercise the right of collective self-defence in support of its US security treaty partner and possibly other US-aligned states in East Asia. Japan's policymakers at this time avoided any type of collective self-defence commitment for fear of entrapment. By the later stages of the Cold War, the issue of collective-self defence was less salient, given that US–Japan security cooperation was concentrated around Japan itself, which meant that any action potential action that Japan took to defend its own territory and US troops in its vicinity could be simultaneously justified under the right of individual self-defence. As the later sections of this chapter and Chapter 4 will argue, Japan's inability to exercise the right of collective-self defence has re-emerged as a key issue for Japan's alliance cooperation with the US, and it now faces strong pressure domestically and internationally to revise its constitutional interpretation.

Japan's exercise of military force has also been governed by a range of anti-militaristic principles and policies, many of which are derived from the Preamble and Article 9 of the Constitution, although they are not constitutionally binding. Table 1 explains these anti-militaristic principles, their origins and the degree to which they were challenged and eroded during the Cold War period.

Table 1 Japan's anti-militaristic principles derived from the Constitution

Japan not to become a military great power ('gunji taikoku to naranai koto')

- Japan's government has regularly repeated this public pledge.
- Japan provides no strict definition of the criteria for this, but stresses that it will not acquire military capabilities above the minimum necessary or that can threaten other states.

Three Non-Nuclear Principles ('hikaku sangensoku')

- Prime Minister Sato introduced the three non-nuclear principles in 1967:
  - Japan is not to produce, possess, or introduce nuclear weapons.
- Japan is to rely instead on the US nuclear umbrella, although it does not regard the possession of its own nuclear deterrent as necessarily unconstitutional if used for the purposes of self-defence.
- The first two principles were strengthened by Japan's entry into the Non-Proliferation (NPT) in 1976.
- The third principle is believed to have been breached by the introduction into or transit through Japanese ports of nuclear weapons on US naval vessels.

Restrictions on the exports of arms and military technology

- In 1967, Prime Minister Sato's administration first enunciated restrictions on arms exports to communist states, countries under UN sanctions, and parties to international disputes.
- In 1976, Prime Minister Takeo Miki's administration ordered restraint in the case of all states, and prohibited the export of weapon-related technology.
- Prime Minister Nakasone partially breached this principle by signing an Exchange of Technology Agreement between Japan and the United States in November 1983.
- Restrictions have largely held, even though Japan has exported certain dual-use technologies with civilian and military applications.
- Since 2003, there have been moves to lift this ban for BMD cooperation.

Peaceful use of space

- In May 1969, the Diet imposed a resolution stating that Japanese activities in space should be limited to peaceful purposes ('heiwa no mokuteki ni kagiri'), interpreted as meaning non-military activities ('higunji').
- Japan's development of spy satellites and a BMD system since the 1990s has challenged this principle. Japan may seek a subtle reinterpretation of this principle, changing the meaning of peaceful purposes to 'defensive' rather than 'non-military', or it may seek to abandon the principle entirely.

One per cent of GNP limit on defence expenditure

- In 1976, Prime Minister Miki established the principle that defence expenditure should be limited to 1% of GNP.
- Prime Minister Yasuhiro Nakasone in effect breached this principle by pushing defence spending just above 1% in 1986.
- Successive administrations have kept Japanese defence spending at around the 1% level.

Civilian control and decision-making

Japan's exercise of military power has been further heavily constrained by the historical memory of pre-war militarism, and the subsequent instigation in the post-war period of the principle of civilian control ('bunmin tosei') over the JSDF. The Japanese Constitution stipulates that all state ministers must be civilians. The JDA and JSDF establishment laws decree that the civilian prime minister is the commander-in-chief of the JSDF and directs the civilian Director General of the JDA, who then gives orders to the uniformed chiefs of staff of the three services of the JSDF. The prime minister is expected to act on behalf of the Cabinet, and in consultation with the National Security Council (NSC) of Japan. In addition, the prime minister must obtain ex-post facto approval from the Diet for the mobilisation of the JSDF. Moreover, the prominence of constitutional issues in shaping Japanese security policy has meant that the Cabinet Legislation Bureau (CLB) ('Naikaku Hoseikyoku'), staffed by elite bureaucrats from a variety of ministries, has played a key role in interpreting Article 9 and its restrictions on the exercise of force.[3] Hence, it is the CLB which has ruled that the JSDF can constitutionally possess nuclear weapons, but that Japan cannot exercise the right of collective self defence.

The framework of constitutional-legal civilian control over the JSDF has been buttressed by one of bureaucratic dominance over the military. Japan's Ministry of Foreign Affairs (MOFA) has traditionally taken overall responsibility for devising security policy. In part, it has been able to maintain this position through its representation on the Security Consultative Committee (SCC), the principal coordinating mechanism for the US–Japan alliance during the Cold War. In contrast, the JDA has traditionally been regarded as a junior partner in security policymaking, regarded as an administrative authority ('kanri kancho') responsible simply for the implementation of policy – unlike full ministries, such as MOFA, which are classified as policy authorities ('seisaku kancho') and are charged with devising as well as overseeing the implementation of policy. The JDA's lack of full ministerial status means that it is incorporated into the Cabinet Office ('Naikakufu') (the government body which supervises the work of agencies and special committees that serve the Cabinet, and until 2001 known as the Prime Minister's Office ['Sorifu']), which in turn is subordinated to the Cabinet, whereas full ministries such as

MOFA report directly to the Cabinet. In addition, many of the JDA's top administrative positions have been 'colonised' by officials from other ministries such as MOFA, the Ministry of Finance (MOF), and the Ministry of Economy, Trade and Industry (METI). The JDA's administrative vice-minister and top bureaucrat is generally a MOF or METI official on secondment.

The JDA, for its part, has exerted a similar structure of civilian bureaucratic dominance ('bunkan tosei') over the JSDF. The internal bureaux ('naikyoku') of the JDA advise the Director General of the JDA, draft legislation for the Cabinet Office and Cabinet, and draft the Director General's instructions to the JSDF's Joint Staff Council (JSC). In effect, the JSC of the JSDF has only an advisory role to the internal civilian bureaux, rather than being directly consulted by other ministries and the civilian leadership, as is the case in other developed states. This has often resulted in tension between JDA bureaucrats and uniformed officers, the latter feeling that they have been sidelined on decisions about military operations, and that the JDA has been concerned more to keep watch over Japan's military to deflect political criticism in the Diet ('kokkai taisaku') than to construct a smoothly functioning national defence policy.

The post-war framework of the subjugation of the military to civilian imperatives was further consolidated by the alienation of the image of the military from Japanese society as a whole. JSDF personnel were encouraged to avoid publicising their profession and to keep a low profile by not wearing uniforms off base. Military careers were accorded low status by the general public, and as a result the JSDF had difficulty in attracting sufficient recruits of sufficiently high calibre. During the Cold War, open discussion of military issues was regarded as taboo, and the JSDF continued to be tarred with the same accusations of militarism as the pre-war imperial army and navy.

Japan's military role has also been limited by the structure of political and executive leadership. The prime minister exercises considerable authority in the management of security affairs by dint of his position at the top of the structure of civilian control. Nevertheless, the ability of Japanese prime ministers to convert this authority into proactive leadership and change in security policy has been circumscribed by a combination of factors. Firstly, the prime minister's formal authority has not always been matched by institutional capabilities within the core executive to facilitate decisive top-down leadership. Japan's core executive, consisting of the Prime Minister's private office and officials from the Cabinet Secretariat ('Naikaku Kanbo') (a parallel body to the Cabinet Office which coordinates the Prime Minister's and Cabinet's relationship with the individual full ministries), physically located within or clustered around the Prime Minister's Official Residence ('Kantei') has traditionally been seen as ineffective in the coordination of security policy, given deficiencies in staff levels, information-gathering abilities and over-reliance on the bureaucracy for relevant expertise.[4] Secondly, Japanese prime ministers have often been beholden to factional politics within the LDP, making the political basis of their authority precarious. Decisions on security have to be made in close consultation with senior LDP officials and faction bosses, the LDP Policy Affairs Research Council (PARC) and its security-focused subcommittees.

Japanese prime ministers have made attempts in the past to strengthen the executive's leadership capabilities. In 1986, a new NSC was created to take the place of the existing National Defence Council, designed to improve coordination between the prime minister and key strategic ministries in ratifying security policy. In the same year, the Cabinet Secretariat was reorganised by adding new posts dealing with foreign and security issues; however, it remained very much staffed and dominated by the key ministries, and thus subject to inter-ministerial rivalries and only loosely controlled by the prime minister.[5] It is also the case that certain prime ministers, bolstered by strong factional or public support, or by the recognition of pressing international circumstances, have been given a freer rein to exercise leadership. Hence, Prime Ministers Yoshida and Kishi were able to negotiate the original and revised security treaties, Sato the reversion of Okinawa and Nakasone to push forward US–Japan alliance cooperation.

In most instances, however, Japan's security policymaking procedures have lacked strong executive leadership and proved highly cumbersome. In terms of overall policy design, the system has been characterised by an emphasis on building consensus among multiple policy agents and heavy reliance on the bureaucracy for the formulation and implementation of policy. In terms of military operability, the necessity of feeding all decisions on the use of military force through the prime minister, at the apex of the policy structure, and the problems in coordinating this process of feeding information upwards, means that the mobilisation of the JSDF is a very slow process.

In many ways, this system has functioned exactly as it was designed to in the post-war period: confirming the principles of civilian control, ensuring an incremental check upon the expansion of security responsibilities and reflecting Japan's general hesitancy towards the use of military power. At the same time, however, and as highlighted by a series of domestic and international security crises following the end of the Cold War, this system does not necessarily enable a flexible or effective response to Japan's perceived changing security needs.

Finally, Japan's security policy, in addition to the structures of civilian control and executive leadership, has been conditioned by the political party system and public opinion. Japan's '1955 political system' ('55nen seiji seido') of LDP, one party governance, ensured considerable continuity in security policy. For close to four decades, successive LDP administrations were able, in a relatively unimpeded fashion, to gradually expand Japan's military capabilities and US–Japan security cooperation. But Japan's opposition parties, even if they could not wrest power from the LDP, did play an important role in constraining developments in security policy. The Social Democratic Party of Japan (SDPJ) maintained a strong opposition to the constitutionality of the JSDF and security treaty throughout the Cold War. If the LDP found that it could not bypass the SDPJ in the Diet, then it was often forced to compensate it in some form by moderating proposed changes in Japan's security policy. For instance, Japan's setting of the ceiling of 1% of GNP for military expenditure was a measure introduced by the government as a trade off for the SDPJ's acceptance of the 1976 NDPO.[6]

In a similar fashion, Japanese public opinion has been important in checking the ambitions of security policymakers. Japanese policymakers have long been aware that security is a domestically explosive issue that could blow apart carefully constructed coalitions among and within political parties, including even the LDP. They have avoided openly transgressing the deep-seated anti-militarism of Japanese society, for fear of provoking a repeat of the political unrest and mass demonstrations (typically involving over half a million participants) seen at the time of the revision of the US–Japan security treaty in 1960 and its indefinite renewal in 1970.

The Japanese government has sought to manage security as a political issue through its incrementalist approach: establishing new precedents in one area of military responsibility and applying this to other areas later, constantly and almost imperceptibly pushing outwards the envelope for the Japanese public's toleration of enhanced military commitments. In addition, these incremental changes have been couched in language which deliberately camouflages and obfuscates their precise implications for Japan's military role, especially vis-à-vis the US–Japan security treaty.[7] Japanese policymakers have been successful in gradually persuading the public of the need to undertake greater military responsibilities, and opinion polls have reflected increasing, if not unambivalent, support for the JSDF's international security role and the maintenance of the US–Japan security treaty.[8] Still, even though public opinion has become less intransigently opposed to changes in Japan's security policy, it is a constant constraint that policymakers must negotiate with the utmost care.

Conclusion

Japan's security role in East Asia during the Cold War, in line with the Yoshida Doctrine, was characterised by an incremental approach to the expansion of military responsibilities and by reliance on the bilateral US–Japan alliance, a highly asymmetrical arrangement providing a mechanism for a mainly indirect contribution to regional military security. Japan's multilateral security involvement in the region was virtually non-existent. Japan's complex policy-making system had an in-built tendency towards 'immobilism' in security affairs.[9] Overall, Japan's security posture was oriented towards the gradual building of cooperation with the US, while avoiding total dependence and entrapment through careful hedging.

Chapter 2

Japan's shifting security trajectory and policy system

Japan's approach towards security policy, its strategic bargain with the US and the assumptions underlying the Yoshida doctrine have undergone significant questioning since the end of the Cold War. This has resulted in a re-intensified debate in Japan on future security options, and moves to accelerate, if not yet fully break, the pattern of incremental change in Japan's security policy; to reconsider the asymmetries of the bilateral alliance; and to assume a more direct role in regional security. The overall consequence has been to set in train fundamental shifts in Japan's post-war security trajectory towards demonstrating greater military proactivity.

Japan's security environment: global, regional, alliance and domestic crises

The Gulf War

Japan's security policy and the Yoshida doctrine first came into question with the collapse of the USSR, which removed the source of threat that had served as the prime rationale for the US–Japan security treaty and the dynamic that forged closer alliance cooperation in the 1980s. However, the subsequent fragility of Japan's security stance and the US–Japan alliance was only to be fully revealed by the 1990–91 Gulf War. Japan failed to respond to US and international expectations that it would provide a 'human contribution' to the war effort of the US-led and UN-sanctioned international coalition. In October 1990, the Japanese government attempted to navigate through the Diet a UN Peace Cooperation Bill that would have enabled the dispatch of a 'UN Peace Cooperation

Corps', composed of volunteer JSDP personnel to the Gulf region for non-combat logistical operations.[1] Stiff opposition in the Diet and poor government preparation scuttled the bill. The government was then obliged to underwrite the war financially with a total contribution of US$13 billion, derided by much of the international community as Japan's standard 'chequebook diplomacy'. Japan was eventually able to dispatch six MSDF minesweepers to the Gulf in April 1991 after the cessation of hostilities, on the grounds that the clearance of mines from sea lanes in peacetime did not represent the exercise of force. The final outcome of this international security crisis, and the subsequent domestic political crisis that it generated in Japan, was to provide momentum for the enactment of the IPCL in June 1992, which has since enabled the dispatch of the JSDF on UN PKO, albeit restricted to logistical and reconstruction activities.

Japan's perceived failure to support its US ally in the Gulf War, and to meet US requests to participate more actively in security at the global level, was the first indication that the status quo in its security policy was no longer tenable and that the US–Japan security relationship was experiencing a crisis of confidence. Japan's next challenge was at the East Asian regional level: that of dealing with expectations of shifting security responsibilities and maintaining the solidarity of the US–Japan alliance in response to the twin security crises involving North Korea and China.[2]

North Korea

North Korea presents for Japan a combination of military threats and, even more worryingly, political threats that unduly magnify these military threats because they complicate the alliance basis of its security policy and revive dilemmas of entrapment and abandonment. Since the early 1990s and in the run-up to the first nuclear crisis of 1994, Japan shared to varying degrees US concerns about North Korea's nuclear programme. Japanese policymakers had also been aware, since the May 1993 test launch of a North Korean *No-dong*-1 missile into the Sea of Japan (East Sea), that a significant part of Japanese territory was exposed to ballistic missile attack from North Korea. In addition, Japan's security establishment feared incursions by North Korean guerrillas into Japan itself to launch attacks on sensitive facilities, such as nuclear power plants. Japanese policymakers clearly preferred a diplomatic resolution to the nuclear issue. But as

US–North Korea tensions escalated in mid-1994, Japan was increasingly pressed to consider military options for dealing with its northern neighbour. It was at this point that North Korea's principal political and military threat to Japan's security became most evident. At the height of the crisis, Japan faced requests from the US for more active and direct support under the bilateral security treaty to apply military pressure on North Korea, including various forms of logistical rear area support (intelligence gathering, extra facilities for the repair of US warships in Japan, and US military use of civilian harbours and airports) and the participation of the JSDF in a naval blockade of North Korea. The Japanese government was unable to respond effectively to these requests: since 1978, under the then instituted US–Japan Guidelines for Defence Cooperation, it had been reluctant to seriously consider Article-6 type bilateral cooperation for regional contingencies. Japan's hesitancy to support its US ally during the nuclear crisis exposed the essential emptiness of the so-called alliance and its lack of military operability to deal with a crisis on the Korean Peninsula or other regional contingencies in the post-Cold War period. Japan's continuing anxieties about entrapment in US-inspired regional wars, and the paralysis that these anxieties induced in the bilateral alliance, led to a full-blown crisis of confidence in the alliance, raising concerns about its future viability and raising the spectre of Japan's abandonment by the US as an unreliable ally.

In the wake of the first and most recent North Korean nuclear crisis, Japan has continued to prefer engagement as the optimum policy towards North Korea. It has committed itself to the support of US moves to engage North Korea via the 1994 Agreed Framework and the Korean Peninsula Energy Development Organisation (KEDO), and supports Seoul's 'Sunshine Policy' of engagement with Pyongyang. Japan has also worked with South Korea to nudge the Bush administration towards negotiations with North Korea, and since December 2003, has participated in the Six-Party Talks on the North Korean nuclear issue. In addition, Japan has sought to engage North Korea bilaterally through attempts to restart diplomatic normalisation talks, the most notable of these being Prime Minister Koizumi's summits with General Secretary Kim Jong-Il in September 2002 and May 2004. These bilateral engagement efforts have been held back by the fact that they must be synchronised with those of the US and South Korea, which have both tended to waver in their commitment to engagement over the past decade. Also, the Japanese government's engagement policy is increasingly hamstrung by growing anti-North Korean domestic sentiment resulting from Pyongyang's admission of its involvement in the abduction of Japanese citizens in the 1970s.

Yet another obstacle to Japan's engagement policy has been the resurgence, since the late 1990s, of the perceived military threat from North Korea. The North's August 1998 launch of a *Taepo-dong*-1 missile over Japanese airspace only served to confirm the fact, long known to policymakers, that Japan was extremely vulnerable to ballistic missile attack. But the incident was highly provocative and heightened the Japanese public's threat perceptions of North Korea. Japanese policymaking and public opinion towards North Korea following the '*Taepo-dong* shock' has been further hardened by the incidents of 'fushinsen' ('suspicious ships') entering Japan's territorial waters. In March 1999, the JSDF intercepted and fired upon two such ships in Japanese waters, believed to be North Korean vessels engaged in routine espionage missions in Japan. This incident was followed by the JCG's interception and pursuit in Japanese waters, and then sinking in Chinese waters, of another North Korean 'suspicious ship' in December 2001. The second nuclear crisis in 2002–03 has compounded Japanese policymakers' concerns about the clear and present dangers manifested by North Korea.

Hence, even while Japanese policymakers explore engagement towards North Korea and attempt to nudge successive US administrations in this direction, they have been forced to counterbalance policies of engagement with those of containment. As a result of the two nuclear crises, which have posed fundamental threats to Japan's security, North Korea has become the most immediate catalyst for the reformulation of Japan's post-Cold War security. As the next chapters will investigate, in responding to the North Korean threat, the Japanese government has sought to minimise the associated risks of entrapment and abandonment by a cautious strengthening of the US–Japan alliance and the augmentation of its own individual national military capabilities.

China

If North Korea represents the most immediate source of threat driving changes in Japan's post-Cold War security policy, then it is

Taiwan – the second major regional crisis zone in East Asia in the post-Cold War period – and the related implications for China's regional security presence that provide the catalyst for changes in Japan's security policy over the longer term.

Japanese policymakers first became concerned about China as a serious military threat in the post-Cold War period. These apprehensions have been occasioned by China's economic rise, and by the qualitative build-up of its armed forces in the wake of the Gulf War. China's upgrading of its strategic nuclear forces is of particular concern: Japan reacted to China's resumption of nuclear testing in 1995 by the suspension of bilateral grant aid. Japanese concerns are heightened not just by the expansion of China's military capabilities per se, but also by the apparent new willingness of China to project military power beyond its immediate borders in support of its national interests. Japan is aware that China could disrupt its SLOCs with only a small blue-water naval capacity and through the assertion of its territorial claims in the South China Sea. China's regular dispatch of 'research ships' and warships into Japan's Exclusive Economic Zone (EEZ) around the disputed Senkaku Islands has been taken as evidence of its aggressive intent.[3] But above all, it was the 1996 Taiwan Strait crisis that raised Japanese suspicions of China's military posture. In attempting to intimidate Taiwan in the run-up to presidential elections, China test-fired ballistic missiles that landed within 60 kilometres of Japan's EEZ around Okinawa. This indicated to Japanese policymakers that China might in future be prepared to launch an invasion of Taiwan and to fight a major war with the US to prevent a Taiwanese declaration of independence. The GSDF has plans for deployment to Okinawa Prefecture in the event of a Taiwan conflict, to prevent the possibility of China invading the islands to disrupt US–Japan military cooperation.[4]

Japan's concerns about conflict in the Taiwan Strait, and the more general potential threat from China, poses major questions for its security policy. In coping with the rise of China, Japan is faced with considerable alliance dilemmas of entrapment and abandonment. Japan could be caught in the middle of a 'tug of war' between the US and China – the most obvious scenario for this being a clash over the Taiwan issue. In this situation, Japan might be pulled dangerously towards one side or the other and enlisted in a political or military conflict for which it is not prepared and wishes to avoid.

Japan's preferred strategy in dealing with a resurgent China is clearly one of political and economic engagement, to avoid turning China into a potential enemy and the risks of entrapment in US military strategy towards China. Nevertheless, the strength of Japan's attachment to the US–Japan alliance as the basis of its security, and its perceived need to manage China's growing power, mean that it will have to avoid the alternative alliance security dilemma of being abandoned by the US as a undependable ally in the event of another Taiwan crisis.

Consequently, from the late-1990s onwards, Japan has been forced into a precarious balancing act, strengthening its own national military capabilities and alliance ties with the US to deal with the rise of China without alienating China. The outcome of this Japanese 'hedging' strategy towards China has been that, even though it is generally acknowledged among most Japanese policymakers that China is the greatest potential military threat to Japan, it is not openly identified as such to avoid unnecessary tensions. Instead, while Japan continues to strengthen its individual and bilateral military options in the event that China should emerge as a potential foe, it persists in identifying North Korea as the principal and most convenient source of threat and legitimisation for the upgrading of its military power.[5]

The 'war on terror'

Changes in Japan's security policy over the medium to longer terms are also driven by the extra-regional international crisis of 11 September and the 'war on terror'. Japan was motivated to respond to the 11 September attacks and the ensuing military campaign in Afghanistan for a number of reasons. First, Japanese policymakers and citizenry share with their US counterparts genuine abhorrence at the terrorism perpetrated by al-Qaeda, and thus a commitment to the expunging of transnational terrorism. Second, the Japanese government has been concerned to avoid a repeat of the 'Gulf War syndrome' and the perception of Japanese failure to make a human contribution to international security. Third, and interrelated with this, has been the fear that any failure by Japan to demonstrate solidarity with its US ally, which now views itself as under direct attack, could again rebound to undermine political confidence in the US–Japan alliance in East Asia and generate risks of abandonment. However, Japan's response to the challenge of 11 September has been tempered by doubts about the utility of military power in dealing with the multi-causal phenomena of terrorism, and concerns that Japan could become entrapped in US military campaigns outside East Asia. For this reason, Japan has, in large part, attempted to articulate a role in the 'war on terror' that relies on the use of economic power, post-conflict reconstruction and state-building practices. Nevertheless, the scale of the international crisis involving the US and the implications for the US–Japan alliance relationship are of such magnitude that Japan has felt obliged to reorient its security policy to involve JSDF out-of-area dispatch in order to support the Afghan military campaign.

The extension of the US's 'war on terror' to Iraq led to a similar adjustment by Japan to enable JSDF out-of-area dispatch in support of the US-led international coalition there; although this has not been conducted without similar doubts regarding the wisdom of such operations. To varying degrees, Japanese policymakers have questioned the legitimacy of the Iraq war in the absence of clear UN mandates; the necessity of using military action and regime change, as opposed to engagement and economic power, in countering the alleged threat from Iraq and other states' WMD; Iraq's actual connections with 11 September and transnational terrorism, and the concept of the 'axis of evil'; the limitations of US capabilities and the feasibility of reconstructing and stabilising post-war Iraq; and the risks of Japanese entrapment in US military adventurism in Iraq and elsewhere in the Middle East. Nonetheless, in the final calculation, Japan's ambivalence has been overridden by concerns about the proliferation of WMD and the alliance imperative of demonstrating support for the US in Iraq to consolidate US support for Japan in countering North Korea, and thereby heading off potential risks of abandonment. Hence, as outlined in more detail in Chapter 5, since the Iraq war Japan has been forced to consider new JSDF missions for the purposes of Iraqi reconstruction, which involve ever higher military risks.

Okinawa

Japanese policymakers' perception of the need to alter the trajectory of post-war security policy has been compounded by a series of security-related domestic crises. The US–Japan alliance jitters that resulted from the first North Korean nuclear crisis were exacerbated in the mid-1990s by renewed domestic opposition in Japan to US bases in Okinawa. Since the island's reversion to Japanese administration in 1972, around 70–75% of US exclusive-use base facilities have continued to be concentrated in Okinawa, with US bases accounting for 10% of the total land area of the prefecture (which constitutes only 0.6% of the entire land area of Japan), and close to 19% of the main island of Okinawa.[6] The necessity for this high concentration of US forces in Okinawa has been questioned since end of the Cold War, and long-term frustration in the prefecture regarding its disproportionate burden of bases reached a critical point with the incident of the rape of a Japanese schoolgirl by three US servicemen in September 1995. The protests of Okinawa Prefecture's government and sizeable sections of its citizenry – culminating in a demonstration on 21 October 1995, attended by 85,000 people, and a prefectural referendum in which a majority of residents voted for the realignment, consolidation and reduction of US bases – shook the US–Japan alliance badly and forced both governments to take action to reduce the burden of bases on Okinawa.

Domestic natural disasters, terrorism and crisis management

Japan's successive failures to cope with the Hanshin-Awaji earthquake in January 1995 and then with the Aum Shinrikyo's (Supreme Truth cult) sarin gas attack on the Tokyo subway in March of the same year, has added further impetus for security policy change. Although the earthquake, which claimed 4,571 lives and injured 14,678 others, was an unpreventable natural disaster, the Japanese government's slow and inadequate response was seen to have accentuated its impact, and as evidence of a general lack of crisis management ('kiki kanri') to deal with not only natural disasters but also, potentially, military threats to Japan. The Aum Shinrikyo's use of a chemical WMD, which killed 11 and injured 3,796, confirmed the deficiencies of Japan's intelligence capabilities and the inability of crisis-management systems to cope with terrorist threats.[7] The Tupac Amaru Revolutionary Movement's occupation of the Japanese ambassador's residence in Peru and the ensuring 127-day siege between 17 December 1996 and 22 April 1997 again raised questions about Japan's preparedness for security threats, which were further confirmed by the accidental sinking by the *USS Greeneville* nuclear submarine of the civilian Japanese training ship, the *Ehime Maru*, on 9 February 2001. Then-Prime Minister Yoshiro Mori, upon first hearing the news, was on the golf course and did not return to his official residence until hours later, leaving the Japanese government in limbo during a diplomatic crisis that could have had dire security implications, given its political impact on confidence in the US–Japan alliance.

Japan's security predicament in the post-Cold War period should not be over-exaggerated: it is still fundamentally one of the most secure states in East Asia, its population and territory largely untouched by direct military conflict over the last 50 years. Moreover, it is clear that Japan's policymakers are not above utilising the various incidents listed above to engender a sense of crisis among the Japanese public in order to legitimise and push forward a more expansive military agenda. Nevertheless, it is clear that the security environment surrounding Japan has become more fluid in the post-Cold War period, posing new challenges for its policymakers and raising public consciousness of the need to ensure national security. The North Korean security issue, the rise of China, the 'war on terror' and various domestic crises have all challenged the basic tenets of Japan's post-war security trajectory. Japan is under increasing pressure to quicken the expansion of its security role; to make a greater 'human contribution' to international security; to equalise its security responsibilities alongside the US; to play a more direct role in East Asian security; and to project military power outside its own region in support of its US ally and the international community. In coping with these often mutually reinforcing, but at times competing, pressures for a new military role, Japan has been obliged to consider ways to revitalise or to adopt new individual national, bilateral and multilateral frameworks for security.

Japan's new security policy debate: towards a 'normal' state?

Japan's 'normalisers'

The first Japanese proponent of an alternative vision of Japan as a more proactive military player or 'normal' state was Ichiro Ozawa, a former LDP powerbroker, leader of a variety of opposition parties and now a member of the Democratic Party of Japan (DPJ). Since the Gulf War, Ozawa has argued that Japan must strive to become a 'normal state' (futsu no kuni).[8] Ozawa posited that Japan, in determining its reaction to the Gulf War, should have taken greater note of the Preamble of the Constitution, which obliges Japan to cooperate with the international community for the purposes of international stability. Under this constitutional interpretation, Japan should have been free to exercise the right of 'international security' ('kokusaiteki anzenhosho'), or 'collective security' to support the US and its other coalition partners in the UN-sanctioned war effort.

'Collective security' is seen to differ from 'collective self-defence' in that the latter is an inherent right under the UN Charter that can be exercised without UN approval in instances where it is deemed necessary to defend another state or ally as if your own territory were attacked, whereas the former is a right that can only be exercised if sanctioned by the UN and is for the purposes of collective retaliation by UN members against an aggressor.[9] Ozawa has argued that the Preamble – preferably combined with a revision of Article 9 to acknowledge Japan's right to maintain military forces for the support of international stability – means that Japan can participate in any form of UN-sanctioned and UN-centred multilateral military operation, from PKO to full-combat peace enforcement and essentially war fighting. Ozawa has also advocated that Japan, while maintaining the US–Japan alliance for the defence of its own immediate territory, should support the creation of a UN standing army and fully participate in such a force as its principal contribution to international security.[10]

Ozawa's concept of a 'normal' Japanese security role and his radical UN-centred collective security option was rejected at the time of the Gulf War, and his presence on the Japanese political scene has ebbed and flowed. Nonetheless, since the early 1990s, the idea of the 'normal' state has been explicitly and implicitly appropriated by other sections of the policy-making community and is now the central reference point for the debate on the future of Japan's security policy. The different sections of policy opinion are united in that they take the developed states of the West as the (often ill-defined or poorly understood) benchmark for 'normalcy' in security policy to which Japan should aspire. Opinion is more strongly divided over how normalisation should be achieved and the relative weight that should be ascribed in this process to greater independent Japanese defence efforts, the strengthening of US–Japan alliance cooperation and the development of multilateral security options.

'Gaullists', the LDP and opposition parties

Japan has a long tradition of 'Gaullist' thinking. In this perspective, the true path towards normality is the removal of constitutional prohibitions on the use of force, the expansion of Japan's independent military capabilities, the equalisation of roles in the US–Japan alliance and the eventual abrogation of the security treaty with the US, as this is the only way to break security dependence on an external power and for Japan to function as a truly independent sovereign state.[11] The best-known advocate of Japanese 'Gaullism' today is the nationalist politician and governor of Tokyo, Shintaro Ishihara, who has long stressed the need for Japan to stand up to the US and to acquire nuclear weapons if necessary.

However, the mainstream of opinion in seeking a 'normal' role for Japan is represented by those in favour of strengthening Japan's individual military capabilities in tandem with a strengthening of the US–Japan alliance. Japan's most influential LDP, MOFA and JDA policymakers have largely held to the position that the pathway towards the normalisation of Japanese security policy is the incremental expansion of national military capabilities and responsibilities within the framework of existing constitutional prohibitions and the US–Japan alliance.[12] At the same time, policymakers have varying degrees of loyalty to this position and differ in their perceptions of Japan's need for a more radical expansion of its military responsibilities individually and in relation to the alliance.

The LDP old guard, which includes senior figures such as Hiromu Nonaka and Shizuka Kamei, and is increasingly fading from the political scene, remains in favour of a highly cautious expansion of Japan's capabilities and alliance cooperation with the US. The current LDP leadership, by contrast to the older generation, has intimated its support for a more radical, or at least accelerated incremental, development of Japan's defence role and the US–Japan alliance. Prime Minister Koizumi himself has indicated that the path to the normalisation of Japan's security policy lies in expanded US–Japan alliance cooperation through the dispatch of the JSDF to the Afghan campaign and to Iraq. Koizumi has expressed personal support for Diet and party political discussions on revising Article 9 of the Constitution and for ending the ban on the exercise of collective self-defence. Koizumi's stance has been backed by Yasuo Fukuda, the

Chief Cabinet Secretary and main government spokesman from 2001 to 2004, often regarded as acting as a de facto second foreign and defence minister. Fukuda has played an important role in urging caution on the LDP and the government in terms of restricting JSDF dispatch to non-combat missions in support of the US 'war on terror' and limiting the geographical scope of dispatch. Fukuda's resignation in May 2004 removed one of the more moderate influential figures in security policy from the government.

Shinzo Abe, a former Deputy Chief Cabinet Secretary and LDP Secretary General and now Acting LDP Secretary General, the number two position in the party, is more radical: strongly in favour of Japan's exercise of the right of collective self defence and known for his hard-line stance against North Korea resulting from the abductions issue. Abe, despite his relative seniority, is representative in part of a younger generation of LDP politicians, both within and without the Koizumi administration, who are vocal in their support for a more 'normal' military stance, for accelerated alliance cooperation and for a reconsideration of existing constitutional restrictions and security taboos. Shigeru Ishiba, the Director General of the JDA from September 2002 until September 2004 – an advocate of stronger independent Japanese defence capabilities, enhanced alliance cooperation, an end to the ban on Japanese weapons exports, the upgrading of the JDA to full ministerial level and the possibility of a preemptive-strike doctrine – represents one strain of this opinion among LDP members. Other younger prominent LDP politicians in favour of the 'normalisation' of Japan's security policy through strengthening the alliance and constitutional revisions, if not as strident as Ishiba, include figures such as Taro Kono.

LDP radicalism in arguing for the normalisation of Japan's security policy should not be overstated. Most 'normalisation' advocates, even those in favour of lifting constitutional restrictions, still adhere to an exclusively defence-oriented policy. Moreover, even LDP politicians who advocate expanded alliance cooperation with the US as a means of security 'normalisation' remain conscious of the risks of entrapment and aware of the need for a more equal relationship, instead of Japan always submitting to US strategic preferences. Indeed, LDP politicians were irked by what they saw as Japan's over-dependence on US satellite capabilities to provide information about North Korea's *Taepo-dong*-1 launch in 1998.

The result was that a number of LDP politicians pushed for Japan to acquire its own satellite intelligence capabilities and to give Japan a stronger voice in discussing security affairs with its US partner.

Nonetheless, while it is important to recognise that the bulk of the LDP remains inherently cautious about overly radical change in Japan's security policy, the party is increasingly committed to a path of 'normalisation' through expanded individual national capabilities and alliance cooperation. Representative of this general shift in LDP attitudes is the 2004 report of PARC's Defence Policy Studies Subcommittee (DPSS), the party's attempt to influence government policy through the ongoing process of revising the NDPO. This report argues that, given the new security environment, Japan should move to amend the Constitution in order to redefine the JSDF as a National Defence Force and provide it with a clear mission for the maintenance and restoration of international peace, one of 'the core aspects of statecraft'.[13] It recommends strongly that Japan should end the ban on collective self defence and tackle the unnecessary 'fear of 'integration' with the forces of other states.[14] The report stresses that these measures should enhance JSDF cooperation with UN activities and, even more significantly, that this will enhance US–Japan bilateral cooperation for 'international peace and stability, opportunities for which could arise in various fields and geographic areas … not limited to the defence of Japan and situations in areas surrounding Japan', thereby hinting at declining concerns about entrapment and the continued expansion of alliance military cooperation beyond the East Asia region and the Japan-US Defence Guidelines.[15] Moreover, the report contains recommendations for according full ministerial status to the JDA; the further restructuring of the JSDF to increase inter-service cooperation and reorientation towards new threats; the introduction of BMD and new command-and-control systems; and the end to the blanket ban on arms exports, to be replaced by a licensing system that prevents exports of weaponry to states affected by UN sanctions or in conflict zones.

LDP commitment to 'normalisation' is only set to grow as the party undergoes generational change and is increasingly dominated by younger members, often with foreign-policy experience acquired overseas, determined to model Japan's security policy on that of other developed states, and with fewer inhibitions about the overt assertion of what they see as Japan's national security interests and the exercise of military force to achieve these. Certain of the younger generation of LDP politicians have been identified as Japan's 'new nationalists', or even 'neo-conservatives'.[16]

The shift in attitudes among policymakers in favour of the 'normalisation' of security has been further promoted by broader changes in the nature of the Japanese political system and opposition politics. In the period 1993–94, domestic political scandals and intra-party factional splits caused the LDP to briefly lose its formerly unbroken 38-year grip on power and it was forced into opposition. Since its return to power in 1994, the party has continued to govern both individually and with a series of coalition partners, the longest serving of which is Komeito, since 1999 to the present day. The LDP's temporary fall from power marked the beginning of the unravelling of the 1955 political system. The increased fluidity of Japanese politics has made it more difficult for the LDP to acquire a firm governing majority in both houses of the Diet. The principal loser from the post-1993 shake up, however, has been the SDPJ. The SDPJ entered into an ill-fated coalition with the LDP from 1994 to 1996, with its leader, Tomiichi Murayama, assuming the premiership. Part of the price of this coalition was the SDPJ's abandonment of its traditional opposition to the constitutionality of the JSDF and the US–Japan security treaty. The eventual outcome was not only the SDPJ's self-abdication as one of the major political checks upon Japanese remilitarisation, but also its eventual near oblivion as a force in the Diet. The SDPJ found itself successively punished by an electorate that felt the party had either sold out on its anti-militaristic principles, or remained too anachronistic in an era of changing security challenges that demanded a more proactive response from Japan.[17]

The SDPJ's place as the main opposition party was eventually taken by the DPJ, formed in 1996 by splinter groups from the SDPJ and smaller parties that had split originally from the LDP, and later on picking up members from a range of other post-1993 parties. The DPJ is broadly centre-left in orientation, and thus has inherited some of the anti-militaristic perspectives of the SDPJ. The SDPJ rump within the DPJ, led by Takahiro Yokomichi, former governor of Hokkaido, and usually consisting of older politicians, has continued to resist constitutional revision and any major extension of Japan's military role.[18] On the fringes of the right wing of the party are more extreme figures such as Shingo Nishimura, who famously, in 1999 as

JDA parliamentary vice-minister, openly questioned if Japan should acquire nuclear weapons and a carrier fleet.

The rest of the DPJ, comprising former LDP members, followers of Ichiro Ozawa and younger politicians more assertive of national interests, such as Shigefumi Matsuzawa and Akihisa Nagashima, has come to support an official policy line that emphasises expanded security responsibilities for Japan, although (reflecting the fragility of consensus with the party) this tends to lack the harder military and bilateral edge of LDP policy. DPJ policy supports the maintenance of the US–Japan security treaty as pivotal to Japan's national security, but also stresses the need for the eventual reduction in the scale of US bases. Former party leader Yukio Hatoyama even went as far, in 2002, as to suggest that Japan might replace the treaty with a mutual defence pact that would not necessitate US bases in Japan. Official party policy has been to support the dispatch of the JSDF to the Afghan campaign (precipitating an open split with the former SDPJ group on the ATSML in the Diet in October 2001), but to oppose JSDF dispatch to Iraq on the grounds that the US-led invasion was not fully legitimised by the UN.

Indeed, the DPJ places more stress on the importance of a UN-centred security policy and the possibilities of multilateral security cooperation in East Asia as a means to lessen dependency on the US–Japan alliance. For instance, in January 2004, then-party leader Naoto Kan suggested the establishment of a special JSDF reserve force to assist in UN operations. This JSDF corps would perform separate functions from forces engaged in US–Japan security treaty cooperation, and thus provide Japan with a role in international peace activities that would not be tied to the US–Japan alliance but which, at the same time, could go beyond existing limited UN PKO. This type of force would thus remove the JSDF from the scope of bilateral alliance cooperation in operations such as Iraq, thereby limiting the risks of entrapment in US strategy outside East Asia. Kan was in part reviving the 1990 concept of a UN Peace Cooperation Corps, as well as adapting Ozawa's notions of collective security and a standing UN reserve force. In July 2004, the new DPJ party leader Katsuya Okada even went as far as to state, controversially, that Japan should be able to exercise force ('buryoku kyoshi') overseas in line with the principle of collective security, premised on a revision of Article 9 of the constitution and UN resolutions.

The issue of security represents the DPJ's 'Achilles heel' in terms of party unity, and the harnessing of its security policy to the legitimacy of the UN offers a means for it to assuage its internal divisions. For example, Yokomichi's group accepted the UN standing force concept as a means to demonstrate Japan's international contribution to security. Meanwhile, the DPJ is wrestling with the issue of constitutional revision: Kan indicated that the party is prepared to investigate all issues connected to constitutional revision and to produce its own draft version for revision in 2006. However, the party is likely to be less forceful than the LDP in pushing for changes to Article 9 and collective self defence.

Hence, the collapse of the 1955 political system has precipitated a fundamental shift in Japanese elite political attitudes towards security policy. Japan's two major political parties are now committed to the maintenance of the US–Japan alliance and increasingly equate Japan's future international security contribution with some form of JSDF overseas dispatch and the exercise of military power, although they still differ over the exact pathway towards 'normalisation'. Moreover, the gap between the LDP and DPJ on security looks set to narrow even further. The increased fluidity and growth of coalition politics in Japan, coupled with the rise of a younger generation of more security-minded and assertive Diet members in both the LDP and DPJ, is creating conditions for greater overlap and convergence in security policy. For instance, the DPJ's current policy chief on security affairs, Seiji Maehara, is in favour of collective self defence, a strengthened bilateral alliance and greater independent defence efforts, and has engaged in bipartisan efforts to revise and pass key security legislation, thereby defying the traditional label of pacifist or hawk and demonstrating a new strain of Japanese 'realist thinking'.[19] Unofficial joint LDP–DPJ study groups for constitutional revision have already come into existence. In fact, rather than the DPJ being the principal obstacle to current LDP security policy initiatives, this role is now falling, somewhat ironically, to the LDP's own coalition partner, the more doveish Komeito. It was Komeito that the LDP had to placate in passing the ATSML and in finding a sufficiently secure area for JSDF dispatch to Iraq; and it may be Komeito that will most effectively resist constitutional revision among the political parties.

Fading alternative visions

Outside the 'normalisation' debate, little space has been created for the consideration of alternative visions of Japan's future security trajectory. In the 1990s, the concept of Japan as a global civilian power ('chikyu minsei taikoku') received considerable attention domestically and internationally. The most influential Japanese champion of this concept was the *Asahi Shimbun* journalist and commentator, Yoichi Funabashi. The concept emphasised that Japan should seek to contribute to international security primarily through economic power, including the distribution of Official Development Assistance (ODA) and building up economic interdependency with East Asia.[20] The concept was important in that it offered a more proactive security policy that suited Japan's obvious economic power capabilities and ambitions for great power status without relying on a further expansion of military commitments. In this way, it resonated with Japanese anti-militaristic traditions and was picked up by certain elements of the policy-making community, such as the economic sections of MOFA, as a rationale for ODA programmes.[21] However, the 'civilian power' concept was not that radical a departure from the 'normalisation' trend: it still advocated the maintenance of the US–Japan alliance as the military basis of Japan's security. The relative waning of Japan's economic power since the late 1990s, coupled with the perceived rise of immediate military threats from North Korea and the 'war on terror' since 11 September, has caused the concept to fade from the mainstream security debate.[22]

Think-tanks, mass media, public opinion

The 'normalisation' debate in Japan has been further spurred by the role of private think-tanks and the mass media. Think-tanks with a security focus, such as the Research Institute for Peace and Security (RIPS) and Institute for International Policy Studies (IIPS), argue for an expanded Japanese security role and strengthened alliance. The Okazaki Research Institute is famed for its fervent support for an upgraded alliance and a fully 'normal' security policy. Even more moderate research institutions, such as the Hiroshima Peace Institute and National Institute for Research Advancement (NIRA), are convinced of the need to reformulate Japan's security policy to grapple with questions of UN PKO, multilateral security cooperation and human security. Japan's media is also increasingly lining up in support, explicitly or implicitly, of normalising of security policy. The *Yomiuri Shimbun* and *Sankei Shimbun* newspapers and media groups favour a stronger defence profile for Japan and constitutional revision. The *Asahi Shimbun*, the leading newspaper and media group on the left of centre, is more critical of current changes to Japan's security policy and the US–Japan alliance. More recently, however, the *Asahi* has become increasingly accepting of the need for a greater Japanese consciousness of national security interests and an expanded contribution to international stability.[23]

Japanese public opinion has by and large come to support, or at least acquiesce, in the push for 'normalisation'. Japanese governmental institutions and media are inveterate pollsters, and there is a wealth of opinion-survey information on attitudes to security policy, although different polling techniques and sample sizes make interpretation problematic. However, the public opinion surveys conducted by the Cabinet Office do offer a relatively consistent set of data that indicate long-term changes in attitudes to security policy from the Cold War to post-Cold War period. The surveys demonstrate that from 1978 to 2003 there was a rise from 48% to 59% in the proportion of the public actively conscious of national security issues.[24] The surveys show a corresponding rise in support for the US–Japan alliance's central role in Japan's security policy. In 1969, 41% of those surveyed were in favour of maintaining the US–Japan security treaty, 13% were in favour of abandoning the treaty and strengthening the JSDF to provide for Japan's independent defence, and 10% were in favour of abandoning the treaty and reducing or disbanding the JSDF. In 2003, 72% were in favour of maintaining the treaty, 8% in favour of an independent defence option for Japan, and 6% in favour of abandoning the treaty and reducing the JSDF.[25] Similarly, public support for JSDF participation in UN PKO has risen strongly. In 1991, 46% were strongly or mildly in favour; by 2003 this had risen to 70%.[26] Overall, Japanese public opinion has shifted in support of the alliance and a greater international contribution to security, keeping in step with elite policy-making opinion. Nevertheless, the polls reveal that Japanese opinion is still highly cautious on security matters. For instance, the majority of opinion has been consistently in favour of maintaining, not increasing, the current levels of JSDF strength and defence expenditure. The public consensus appears to be that the JSDF's most important function to date has been the response to domestic natural disasters such as earthquakes and floods, the national defence function being of secondary importance; and that the JSDF's international contribution should be made via the UN.[27]

The shift of public opinion in favour of a more 'normal' security role has empowered Japanese policymakers, who have felt increasingly emboldened to launch new security initiatives. Moreover, certain key policymakers and certain key events have generated public support for the expansion of Japan's military role. Prime Minister Koizumi's extraordinary level of public support since taking office (obtaining around 80–90% approval in the first stages of his appointment, but since settling at around 50%) has helped him overcome domestic opposition and respond to the 'war on terror' through the dispatch of the JSDF to the Indian Ocean and Iraq. The 'war on terror' itself has clearly affected Japanese public opinion's consciousness of security policy. In the immediate post-11 September period, most opinion polls showed a sizeable majority in favour of JSDF dispatch to support to the US and the international community to counter terrorism, although the preferred role for the JSDF was a non-combat and logistical one. Japanese opinion has been more divided over the Iraq war. Most opinion polls showed public opposition to the US-led invasion of Iraq, but later, support for JSDF dispatch on non-combat reconstruction missions, provided that a genuine non-combat zone could be found for their activities. In particular, the legitimisation of these operations by allusion to UN resolutions was an important consideration for boosting support for JSDF dispatch – again demonstrating the essential caution of public opinion on security issues.

Shifts in Japanese public opinion have been crucial in expanding the realm of possibilities for security policy in recent years, and paved the way for expanded US–Japan alliance cooperation, UN PKO and JSDF dispatch to the Indian Ocean and Iraq. Having said that, Japanese public opinion remains a significant check on policymakers' ambitions, and in launching new initiatives they are always obliged to consider how to legitimise government actions in the eyes of the public. This often – as will be seen later – involves calling upon UN legitimacy and the skilful stretching of constitutional interpretations so as not to overly disturb mass opinion.

Japan's newly proactive policy-making system

Japan's changing international environment and domestic debate on security have created the conditions for an expanded and more 'normal' security role. In turn, the transformation of the Japanese security policy-making system, triggered by these changes, is now enabling a more active security role for Japan.

'Normalisation' of the JDA and JSDF's policy role

MOFA retains overall responsibility for the formulation of Japan's security policy and, in line with the principle of civilian control, continues to be cautious about ascribing the military too great a role in security planning and is wary about the commitment of Japanese forces to combat situations. But MOFA is aware of the need for Japan to fulfil greater security responsibilities, and has sought to expand Japan's cooperation with the US as far as possible within constitutional limitations and without irreversibly committing itself to US strategy in East Asia. MOFA has also shown a keenness to dispatch the JSDF on UN PKOs and in US-led coalitions in the Indian Ocean and Iraq to demonstrate Japanese solidarity with the international community and its bilateral ally.

However, MOFA's leading role in security planning is increasingly being eroded by political and bureaucratic competition. Since 2001, MOFA has suffered from high-profile corruption scandals and internal wrangling between officials and ministers, most notably involving former Foreign Minister Makiko Tanaka.[28] The result has been that the ministry, traditionally weak in the political system, has been pilloried by the media and political parties, lost key personnel and often been left debilitated by the policy-making process. Moreover, MOFA has been forced onto its political back foot by strong public criticism that it allegedly appeased North Korea over the abductions issue.

MOFA faces increased competition from the JDA as it begins to upgrade and 'normalise' its role in the making of security policy. The JDA has continued to carefully oversee the JSDF, but has pushed for a greater regional role for Japan's military in UN PKO and especially in support of the US. In September 1996, the SCC was reconstituted to include the Japanese Minister of Foreign Affairs and the Director General of the JDA, and the US Secretaries of State and Defence. In this '2+2' formula, the JDA has derived increased legitimacy by equalising its role relative to MOFA in negotiating with the US. In a sign that the JDA is taken increasingly seriously, it has relocated from its dilapidated site in Roppongi to a state-of-the-art headquarters in the Ichigaya district of Tokyo, and has routinely pressed for status as a full ministry that would wield influence comparable with its peers. Younger JDA career bureaucrats – well-versed in defence matters, often graduates from elite universities and with graduate-school experience in international relations programmes in the US, and prepared to work with the JSDF for the protection of what they see as vital national security issues – are now beginning to assume the most senior positions within the JDA.[29] However, the JDA's rise has not gone unchecked. Its desire for full ministerial status is still resisted by many policymakers, and its image has suffered from procurement scandals in the late 1990s and from JDA officials' illegal collection, in 2002, of personal data on members of the public who had requested access to agency information.

The JSDF, for its part, generally favours a more active security role. The MSDF's close working relationship with the US Navy, built up since the Cold War, means that it seeks closer cooperation still with the US in areas such as the patrolling of SLOCs, logistical support for regional crises and BMD. The ASDF also wishes for a greater role in supporting US power-projection capabilities in regional contingencies, and the capabilities to support JSDF PKO. The GSDF has a less defined role post-Cold War, given the demise of the threat of a Soviet land invasion. However, it still wishes for closer working co-operation with the US, and an expanded role in UN PKO, as long as this does not mean dispatch to regions where they are exposed to combat situations for which they are not equipped, given constitutional prohibitions on the use of force. The JSDF has been able to make common cause with the JDA in pushing forward Japan's military role, given its own increasingly 'normalised' role in the policy process, in large part resulting from enhanced legitimisation gained from participation in UN PKO and a deliberate campaign to raise its public image.[30] The JSDF's image was briefly tarnished by a spy scandal in 2000, involving an MSDF officer passing confidential documents to Russian intelligence agents.

Since the abolition of the 1952 National Safety Agency Order in 1997, JSDF officers are now allowed to testify in the Diet and have improved access to the Cabinet Office, Cabinet and Kantei to offer direct advice on security affairs.[31] The principle of civilian control has also undergone a subtle change since 2003. The JDA's *Defence of Japan* White Paper has deleted the wording that explicitly stated that the civilian Administrative Vice-Minister and Defence Counsellors assist in the creation of basic defence policy. The JSDF pushed for this change to diminish the influence of the oversight of middle-ranking 'naikyoku' over the military, and to open up a more direct route for JSDF officers to provide advice on security policy to the Director General of the JDA.[32]

The JSDF's improved image, combined with the effect of the economic downturn in Japan, has also meant that, for the first time, it has an excess of suitable applicants. An additional boost to the JSDF's normalisation has been provided by its ever closer links with the US military. The JSDF and US military, working in tandem, have been able to apply bottom up pressure on the policy system for the enhancement of the Japanese military's voice in policymaking, thus complementing the increasing penetration of the policy system by the US at the government-to-government level.

Koizumi and the 'normalisation' of the role of the core executive

Japan's security policy-making system has further been characterised by the greater 'normalisation' of control by the core executive located in the Kantei. Koizumi's extraordinary popularity has already been cited as a crucial factor in boosting executive leadership over security policy. Koizumi has been able to use his public mandate to carry the LDP party and elements of the opposition parties with him in the decisions to dispatch the JSDF to the Afghan campaign and to Iraq. Moreover, Koizumi has used the extra authority derived from his personal popularity to cow potential bureaucratic opposition from the CLB to those features of JSDF dispatch that stretched constitutional restrictions – such as support for the war in Afghanistan – thereby creating greater room for executive action in extending Japan's military role.[33] Koizumi, like many of his predecessors, has sought to strengthen his independent decision-making capacity by drawing on policy advice from outside the main government ministries. He appointed Yukio Okamoto, a former MOFA official, to act as the Prime Minister's and Cabinet's special advisor on foreign and security affairs (Okamoto served from 2001 to

2004), and visited Iraq on a fact-finding mission on behalf of Koizumi). In September 2004, Taku Yamasaki, a close ally of Koizumi, was appointed as a special advisor on security issues. Koizumi has also appointed prime ministerial commissions composed of academics and business leaders to produce reports related to security policy. These commissions have included the Advisory Group for International Cooperation on peace, headed by Yasushi Akashi, former Under Secretary General of the UN, reporting in November 2002; and the Task Force on Foreign Relations, headed by Okamoto and reporting in December 2002.[31]

Even more importantly, Koizumi's influence has been bolstered by reforms of the core executive structure instituted since 2001. The revised Cabinet Law of 1999 clarified the prime minister's authority to propose key policies at Cabinet meetings, with the effect of strengthening the prime minister's top-down executive leadership while diluting the traditional bottom-up style of Japanese decision-making. The Cabinet Secretariat that forms part of the Kantei and core executive structure was reorganised by the merging of the three previous policy offices of Internal Affairs (headed by a MOF official), External Affairs (headed by a MOFA official) and National Security Affairs and Crisis Management (headed by a JDA official) into one Office of Assistant Chief Cabinet Secretaries, led by three Assistant Chief Cabinet Secretaries. The aim of this reform was to remove the ministerial sectionalism prevalent under the old structure and introduce a Cabinet Secretariat capable of dealing in a flexible and integrated manner with complex issues by drawing on personnel from multiple ministerial backgrounds and expertises.[35] In addition, in 1998, the position of Deputy Chief Cabinet Secretary for Crisis Management, head of the Office of Crisis Management, was established, and charged with the role of enhancing government coordination to respond to natural disasters and domestic and internal security crises.

The importance of these structural reforms in boosting the decisiveness and rapidity of Kantei core executive leadership was demonstrated by the Japanese government's response to 11 September. Only 45 minutes after hearing of the attacks, Koizumi was able to establish a liaison office ('Kantei Renrakushitsu') at the Office of Crisis Management, later the same day converted to an emergency response office ('Kantei Taisakushitsu'), and then on 8 October upgraded to the Emergency Anti-Terrorism Headquarters ('Kinkyu Tero Taisaku Honbu'). The office was led by Chief Cabinet Secretary Fukuda and Deputy Chief Cabinet Secretaries Shinzo Abe and Teijiro Furukawa from the Cabinet Secretariat. On 13 September, Furukawa instigated a secret task force, headed by Assistant Chief Cabinet Secretary Keiji Omori on transfer from the JDA and consisting of key officials from MOFA, the JDA and CLB, to oversee government policy.[36] Close cooperation within the Cabinet Secretariat enabled the government to announce its Basic Policy in response to 11 September only eight days later, on 19 September, including the proposal to dispatch the JSDF to provide support for US and other forces in actions against terrorism. Following these announcements, on 5 October, the Japanese government submitted the ATSML to the Diet and it entered into law by 29 October.

The contrast with previous security crises, such as the Gulf War, is striking and suggests that the Koizumi's leadership in pushing through significant changes to Japan's security policy is not a flash-in-the-pan phenomenon dependent on his public popularity. Increasingly, Japan is acquiring a 'normal' core executive with the administrative structure and expertise to coordinate different ministries and the political parties in the Diet, and concomitantly to take on a more 'normal' international security role. During the Iraq war, Japan's core executive was able to repeat this feat of rapid and coordinated policymaking. The 11 September task force model was replicated in the Cabinet Secretariat to ensure smooth information sharing among the Deputy Chief Cabinet Secretaries, MOFA and JDA.[37]

Constitutional revision?

The final component of change in the policy-making system that opens the way for Japan to assume a 'normal' military role is constitutional revision. As noted above, the new atmosphere surrounding security in Japan has meant that constitutional revision has ceased to be a taboo. Since January 2000, Constitutional Research Commissions in the House of Representatives and House of Councillors have conducted substantive investigations into constitutional revision, including the issue of Article 9. The expectation is that the research committees will submit final reports in May 2005, and judging from the tone of discussions, as summarised in the mid-term report of 2002, there is strong support for revision of Article 9 to specify the existence of the JSDF as a military force, and to clarify the right of collective self-defence and legitimise the JSDF's role in international cooperation with the US and UN.[38] As already pointed out, the LDP's leadership is in favour of constitutional revision along these lines; the LDP's PARC has established an internal Research Commission on the Constitution, which is expected to stress similar revisions in its November 2005 report. The DPJ has initiated its own research team to report on constitutional revision by 2006, and, while its findings are expected to be less radical than the LDP's, it still opens the way for more general acceptance of the need for revision. According to a poll in July 2004, prior to elections for the House of Councillors, 62% of all candidates condoned the idea of constitutional revision (including 100% of LDP candidates and 77% of DPJ candidates in favour).[39] If proposals finally come forward for revision, they will still require a steep two-thirds majority in the Diet for their implementation, as well as the creation of a law to enable a public referendum on the issue. Nevertheless, it is clear that constitutional revision, previously unthinkable, has arrived as an immediate political issue. Given changes in public attitudes, the trend for bipartisan cooperation on security policy, and the increasing skill of the government and LDP in piloting controversial security legislation through the Diet, *de jure* constitutional revision may become a reality very soon. In any case, and as pointed out in Chapter 5 dealing with dispatch to Afghanistan and Iraq, de facto constitutional reinterpretation is already underway, enabling the government to implement significant changes to security policy without needing to wait for the ultimate sanction provided by constitutional revision. Hence, constitutional revision may, in the end, only be an exercise in squaring legal regulations with the on-going military reality, rather than being the point of initiation for a greater Japanese military role.

Conclusion

Japan's security policy is on the march. Under the influence of the Yoshida doctrine, policymakers remain wary of the risks of overseas military entanglements and entrapment in US military strategy, and continue to pursue a cautious incremental approach to expanding security responsibilities. Nonetheless, a series of international crises, from the Gulf War to the Iraq war, have pushed Japan's policymakers to diverge from the Yoshida doctrine and move towards accepting the need to accelerate the pace of change in security policy, to expand direct military cooperation as a 'normal' ally with the US in East Asia and beyond, as well as with the UN. Japan's reformed policy-making system is able to countenance and realise a more proactive military role. The increasing consensus in Japan among the political parties, bureaucracy, military and the public is that Japan should seek to become a more 'normal' military player in international security. The concurrent 'normalisation' of the JDA, JSDF and executive control has made the realisation of this vision increasingly possible. Moreover, these shifts in the trajectory of Japan's post-war security policy are likely to be sustained long term, fashioned as they are by deep international and domestic forces. The following chapters will examine how these changing security policy attitudes and structures have been played out over the last decade in terms of the development of Japan's individual national security policy, bilateral alliance cooperation with the US and multilateral security cooperation.

Chapter 3

Japan's national security policy and capabilities

Japan is adapting its national security policy to the post-Cold War security environment through the revision of its military doctrines, the introduction of new security legislation and the acquisition of new military hardware. In certain ways, Japan's evolving national security doctrine and capabilities provide it with latent options for an expanded independent and multilateral security role. Nevertheless, it is clear that Japan's national security policy is still very much designed in conformity with, and to strengthen, the US–Japan bilateral alliance.

National Defence Programme Outline revision

Japan's first fundamental attempt to address the new security complexities of the post-Cold War period was the 1995 revision of the 1976 NDPO. The original NDPO was devised in the period of detente and, for the first time, set out the principles for Japan's defence alongside the necessary force structure to achieve these. The NDPO stated that Japan would maintain a force structure to enable it in the first instance to repel limited direct aggression by itself, but that in cases where this aggression proved too great, the force structure would be capable of effective resistance until US cooperation was forthcoming. The necessary denial capabilities ('boshiryoku') for Japan's defence were defined as a 'standard defence force concept' ('kibanteki boeiryoku koso'). This force structure was intended to provide the nucleus of a qualitatively improved and minimum defence posture for the JSDF in a period of detente and peacetime, which could be adapted in a relatively short time-span to repel various types of direct aggression against Japan. The 'standard defence force' concept differed from that of the 'required defence force' ('shoyo boeiryoku'), which had influenced the previous quantitative and qualitative build-up of the JSDF in the immediate post-war period. The 'required defence force' dictated that force levels were capable of matching, in a balance-of-power type fashion, extant regional capabilities that could be employed for aggression against Japan. In the case of Japan and East Asia, the 'required defence force' structure, if not abandoned in the 1976 NPDO, could have meant the relentless build-up of the JSDF to attempt to match Soviet regional capabilities.

The NDPO and the 'standard defence force' concept had considerable utility for Japan's policymakers in an era of detente. Even in a time of relaxed international tensions, Japan was able to proceed with a qualitative build-up of the JSDF and to re-emphasise the importance of the US–Japan security arrangements to obviate any risk of abandonment. Simultaneously, the 'standard' defence force concept was employed to restrict the potentially endless quantitative build-up of the SDF and defence expenditure for which there was limited domestic support.

Soon after its release, the 1976 NDPO faced immediate criticism from the JSDF for rejecting the 'required defence force' in favour of the 'standard defence force' concept. The JSDF claimed that the NDPO had underestimated the size of forces necessary to counter Soviet influence after the waning of detente in the latter half of the Cold War. In the post-Cold War period, the NDPO came under further criticism from Japan's security policy community for bequeathing to Japan a military force structure more suited to the exigencies of the bipolar struggle than to the more fluid security environment of the 1990s.

In response to these criticisms, the Japanese government initiated a review of the NDPO. August 1994 saw the publication of the report of the Prime Minister's Advisory Group on Defence, known as the Higuchi Report after its chairman. The report characterised the post-Cold War security environment as one in which bipolar conflict had given way to diverse and non-specific problems, including regional tensions involving the Korean Peninsula and China; intra-state conflict in Cambodia; the proliferation of WMD; and economic insecurity. The report recommended that Japan should respond not only by strengthening the US–Japan alliance, but also by taking initiatives to increase JSDF UN PKO participation, and by promoting multilateral security dialogue in East Asia. The report, if fully acted upon, could have produced a significant shift in Japan's military security towards greater multilateral cooperation.

Many innovative features of the Advisory Group's report were fed into the process of revising the NDPO at the official MOFA and JDA level. The revised NDPO of November 1995 took a similar view of the international strategic environment. Like the Higuchi Report, it stressed the importance of strengthening the US–Japan alliance, the enhancement of bilateral and multilateral security dialogue, and greater JSDF participation in UN PKO, as well as hinting at a new anti-terrorism role for the JSDF. The revised NDPO's indication of new directions for Japanese security policy, though, was balanced by the reaffirmation of traditional security principles (including the concept of the 'standard defence force') and the essential conservatism of the defence establishment. Despite the fact that the NDPO recognised that the JSDF needed to be more compact and flexible to deal with emerging low-intensity conflicts and made cuts in frontline equipment, it still retained large numbers of interceptor aircraft, anti-submarine warships and main battle tanks acquired during the Cold War (Table 2).

In addition, the NDPO was designed to strengthen the US–Japan alliance after the first North Korean nuclear crisis, and its promotion of Japan's role in multilateral security dialogue was predicated on a toughened alliance as the platform for such activity. The revised NDPO makes frequent reference to the importance of the US–Japan security system ('Nichibei anzen hosho taisei'), which is mentioned 13 times, by contrast to the three mentions in the original NDPO text. The revised NDPO overturns part of the defence doctrine of the original – now stating that Japan will, in the event of any form of direct aggression, seek from the outset to repel this with the assistance of the US. The revised NDPO further departed from the original by inserting a new clause to state that if a situation should arise in areas surrounding Japan ('shuhen') that 'impacts upon' national peace and security, then Japan would seek to deal with this in line with constitutional restrictions and through support for UN activities, and the smooth implementation of US–Japan security arrangements. The intention of the NDPO's framers was to demonstrate that Japan would now seek actively to support US military forces to function not just in the defence of Japan but of the surrounding region. This drew on the purport of the unfinished research on US–Japan cooperation for regional contingencies under the 1978 Defence Guidelines, thus preparing the way for the next revision of the Guidelines and for Japan to expand its potential role in supporting the US in regional contingencies.[1] In sum, the revised NDPO was a statement of Japan's individual national security doctrine, but it was also very much tied to the needs of bilateral cooperation with the US.

The NDPO has remained in force since 1995, but its relatively modest reforms of the JSDF's post-Cold War force structure and role has meant that the Japanese government is already preparing for another revision in late 2004 or early 2005. Koizumi instructed the JDA to begin the review in December 2003, following extensive internal discussions since 2001 by the JDA's Defence Posture Review Board. In April 2004, similar to the 1995 revision, a Prime Minister's Council on Security and Defences Capabilities was established, comprising a range of business figures, academics, former bureaucrats and JSDF officers. The council published its final report at the start of October 2004, and some of its recommendations may be fed into the JDA's revision of the NDPO.[2] It was notable in calling for an 'Integrated Security Strategy' for Japan that would mandate a two-pronged role for the JSDF: a traditional function of preventing direct threats from impacting on Japan; and a new emphasis on international cooperation outside Japan's territory to prevent the rise of security threats. The report, amongst other proposals, also called for the strengthening of information gathering and exchange amongst relevant security actors in Japan; the strengthening of the NSC functions; the introduction of BMD; improved US–Japan defence cooperation; and a more flexible stance on arms exports. The report fudged the issue of constitutional revision, calling for more investigation but that Japan should at least settle its position quickly on collective self defence.

Final NDPO revision in 2004–05 will take into account a number of issues. Firstly, the need for continued JSDF restructuring is likely to mean new reductions in frontline equipment that does not serve the purposes of an expanded Japanese role in international security cooperation with the US and in UN PKO. Significant numbers of GSDF main battle tanks, ASDF interceptor aircraft, and MSDF surface ships may become surplus to requirements – it is rumoured that the NDPO will cut around 300 tanks, to reduce the number of F-2s to be introduced to 100 from 130, and to decommission six destroyers.[3] The NDPO's push for Japan's procurement of a BMD system (a call also made in the Prime Minister's council group) and its colossal cost is only likely to add to the pressure for cuts in Cold War-style conventional weaponry.

Secondly, NDPO revision is likely to consider the abandonment or revision of the 'standard defence force' concept as too rigid to take account of the rapidly changing security environment, and adopt instead the type of concept outlined in the Prime Minister's council's report of a 'multi-functional and flexible force'.[4] Japan appears interested in the UK 1998 Strategic Defence Review as a possible model, and in the creation of JSDF rapid reaction forces for service overseas and for joint operations between the GSDF, MSDF and ASDF – a feature noticeably weak in JSDF planning over the last 50 years. Indeed, the JDA may even call, controversially, given constraints on defence spending, for an expansion of GSDF troop numbers by 7,000 in order to create a standby force exclusively for overseas dispatch, and able to deploy two units of 1,300 each to different locations simultaneously. Japan may also adopt elements of a 'required defence force' concept that would give Japan greater flexibility to match extant threats as well as opening the way for the build-up of certain key capabilities.

Thirdly, NDPO revision will likely result in the elevation of UN PKO to become a primary mission of the JSDF. Fourthly, the JSDF is likely to acquire a more prominent role in counter-terrorism; one that is likely to cause some friction with the National Policy Agency (NPA), which has usual responsibility for this task. The JDA and JSDF have been deadlocked over a number of issues, in particular, inter-service disputes over the loss of frontline equipment. The Prime Minister's Council on Security and Defence Capabilities was in part established to help break this deadlock and to strengthen the Kantei's authority over security policymaking.[5] However, the resignation before the report's production of Chief Cabinet Secretary Fukuda, the council's principal political sponsor, may weaken its impact, so returning the initiative on NDPO revision to the JDA and JSDF. The JDA will still face, though, a fierce battle against MOF to attain its

Table 2 **Equipment and personnel numbers under 1995 and 1976 NDPOs**		
	1995 NDPO	**1976 NDPO**
SDF personnel	160,000	180,000
regular personnel	145,000	
ready reserve personnel	15,000	
GSDF		
major units		
regionally deployed units	8 divisions	12 divisions
	6 brigades	2 combined brigades
mobile operation units	1 armoured division	1 armoured division
	1 airborne brigade	1 airborne brigade
	1 helicopter brigade	1 helicopter brigade
ground-to-air missile units	8 anti-aircraft artillery groups	8 anti-aircraft artillery groups
main equipment		
battle tanks	approximately 900	approximately 1,200
artillery	approximately 900	approximately 1,000
MSDF		
major units		
destroyer units (for mobile operations)	4 flotillas	4 flotillas
destroyer units (regional district units)	7 divisions	10 divisions
submarine units	6 divisions	6 divisions
minesweeping units	1 flotilla	2 flotillas
land-based patrol aircraft units	13 squadrons	16 squadrons
main equipment		
destroyers	approximately 50	approximately 60
submarines	16	16
combat aircraft	approximately 170	approximately 220
ASDF		
major units		
aircraft control and warning units	8 groups	28 groups
	20 squadrons	1 squadron
	1 squadron *(airborne early-warning squadron)*	
interceptor units	9 squadrons	10 squadrons
support fighter units	3 squadrons	3 squadrons
air reconnaissance units	1 squadron	1 squadron
air transport units	3 squadrons	3 squadrons
ground-to-air missiles units	6 groups	6 groups
main equipment		
combat aircraft	approximately 400	approximately 400
fighters *(included in combat aircraft)*	approximately 300	approximately 350

Source: Boeichohen, *Boei Hakusho* (Tokyo: Okurasho Insatsukyoku, 1995), pp. 312, 321.

desired force numbers. MOF, eager to save costs, is believed to want to cut the GSDF task force by half, cut GSDF troop levels from 160,000 to 120,000, and reduce MSDF destroyers by twelve.

National emergency legislation

Japanese memories of the imperial military's domination of domestic politics and mobilisation of the population to serve its ends during the pre-war and wartime periods, combined with the low probability of direct invasion, meant that during the Cold War, the government was careful about attempting to acquire crisis-management powers to subordinate the civilian sector to the needs of the military. In 1978, the JDA began research into emergency and crisis legislation ('yuji hosei') to provide the government with the enhanced control over the requisitioning of civilian land and buildings, electrical power networks and transport systems. The research stalled because of inter-jurisdictional disputes among related ministries, concern about public reaction, and the decline of visible threats to Japan with the end of the Cold War.

Japanese interest in emergency legislation was rekindled by the first North Korean nuclear crisis, the Aum Shinrikyo sarin attacks and the Hanshin-Awaji earthquake, all of which highlighted deficiencies in government crisis management and the restrictions on the JSDF and other security authorities' ability to respond to major emergencies. Japanese policymakers were concerned that the JSDF did not have a sufficient legal mandate to respond to the threat of North Korean guerrilla incursions against nuclear power plants on the Sea of Japan coastline. Moreover, the lack of emergency legislation was also thought to hinder the JSDF's ability to mobilise in support of US forces in contingencies directly affecting Japan or in the surrounding region, as stipulated in the US–Japan Defence Guidelines. Consequently, following the start of Defence Guidelines revision from September 1997, the government resumed research into emergency legislation to deal with issues such as the evacuation of Japanese nationals resident abroad, the guarding of coastal installations and the management of refugee flows. Research was again impeded by JDA–NPA disputes over which ministry should take responsibility for anti-guerrilla duties, and concerns that there was little public appetite for accepting further security legislation following the formulation of the controversial revised Defence Guidelines.

After 24 years of study, the Japanese government finally submitted emergency and crisis legislation for Diet consideration in April 2002, in the shape of 'three bills to respond to armed attack' ('Buso Kogeki Jitai Taisho Kanren Sanpo' – Law Concerning Measure to Ensure National Independence and Security in a Situation of Armed Attack; Law to Amend the Security Council Establishment Law; Law to Amend the Self Defence Forces Law). The impetus for submission was provided by the events of 11 September and the December 2001 incursion of North Korean spy ships into Japanese waters, all creating an enhanced perception of the JSDF's need to be better equipped to deal with terrorism and insurgency.

The three bills included measures to strengthen the prime minister's authority to coordinate the defence against armed attacks by forming a task force to direct the efforts of central and local government, and by the streamlining of the National Security Council decision-making. The JSDF was provided with new authority in times of attack to expropriate private property and construct defensive facilities on private land, and a number of laws were relaxed to allow the military greater freedom to deploy and to provide medical treatment to civilians.

The initial passage of the bills through the Diet, however, was not smooth. In a rare example of the Diet exercising its prerogatives in the post-Cold War period, it sought major modifications to the legislation. The LDP, Komeito and DPJ, although sharing a general cross-party consensus in favour of national emergency legislation, were concerned that the conditions for JSDF mobilisation lacked specificity. The parties argued that the original condition for JSDF mobilisation – 'predicted armed attack' – could trigger deployment in nearly any kind of scenario, and insisted instead that the condition be split into an actual 'situation of armed attack' and a situation where 'armed attack is predicted', so as to force the government to make the rationales for deployment clearer. In addition, despite the fact that the government made clear its intention to submit, at a later date, another round of legislation specifically to outline measures for JSDF mobilisation to support the US in regional crisis situations, the bills currently under consideration were viewed more as measures to complement the revised Defence Guidelines than to facilitate Japan's national defence. JSDF mobilisation in the three bills appeared more concerned with measures to assist in a straight conventional war, rather than concentrating on fighting terrorism and insurgency – supposedly the bills' principal justification post-11 September. The government was obliged to modify the bills to state that they were designed to deal with new threats, such as large-scale terrorism and incursions of 'fushinsen'.[6] Lastly, the powers provided to the government and military, including the right to fine or imprison civilians who obstructed JSDF activities, were viewed as too sweeping. The government was forced to promise complementary legislation that would guarantee civilian rights in a time of emergency. Following these modifications, the Diet passed the bills in June 2003 with a nearly 90% vote in favour.

Between March and June 2004, the Japanese government passed a further seven national emergency legislation bills relating to armed attack upon Japan through the Diet. The first bill was concerned with national and local government measures to protect citizens in case of an attack on Japan, such as large-scale terrorism, including measures for evacuation and the provision of food and medical aid. Three bills dealt with the JSDF's treatment of prisoners of war and other behaviour under international law, and established the prime minister's authority to enable the JSDF and US military to use civilian seaports, airports, roads, and radio and telecommunication facilities. The last three bills focus on enhancing US–Japan security cooperation, including: new powers for the prime minister to allow US forces to requisition private land and buildings; MSDF powers to inspect, without crew or owner consent, foreign ships in Japan's territorial waters suspected of carrying military items; and a revision to the Self Defence Forces Law enabling the JSDF to supply US forces with ammunition in the event of an attack on Japan.[7] This last bill complemented the signing of the revised US–Japan Acquisition and Cross Servicing Agreement (ACSA) on 27 February 2004, which expanded the range of scenarios in which Japan would provide logistical support to the US.

Finally, the Japanese government has augmented its crisis management by the passing in October 2001 of a law to enable the JCG to fire upon intruder vessels, given certain conditions: that the intruder vessel represents a danger to security within Japan's territorial waters; that there is a probability that the vessel will repeat the act if not dealt with; that the vessel is suspected of committing a serious crime; and that it is not possible to stop and search the vessel.

Acting under this new law, the JCG fired upon and eventually sunk a North Korean vessel in December 2001. This collection of emergency legislation demonstrates that Japan is now contemplating more seriously than at any time in the previous half-century the possibility that it needs to ready itself for war fighting.

Japan's military hardware: pursuing power-projection capabilities
Defence expenditure

As a result of the 1995 NDPO revision, the JSDF has undergone a quantitative build-down of its Cold War-style capabilities, a trend that will likely be consolidated by NDPO revision in 2005. The JSDF has attempted to compensate by the qualitative build-up of its capabilities to address the new security environment. Japan's drive to acquire new quantitative capabilities has been constrained by its economic downturn since the early 1990s and the concomitant pressure to limit defence expenditures. If measured in nominal US dollar terms, the total Japanese defence budget has continued to rise strongly even after the end of the Cold War – standing at US$40bn in 2001, only second to that of the US. But these figures are inflated by the strength of the yen against the dollar. If Japan's defence budget is calculated in nominal Japanese yen, then it can be seen to have stagnated and fractionally fallen since 1997.[8] This contrasts strongly with the 1980s and early 1990s, when the annual rate of increase was between 5% and 7%. Since the late 1990s, the fall in the value of yen has produced a fall in the dollar value of Japan's defence budget. The ¥5 trillion yen budget seems to have been accepted as a de facto

Chart 1 **Japan's Defence Expenditure 1975–2003 (US$, nominal)**

Source: International Institute for Strategic Studies, *The Military Balance* (Oxford: Oxford University Press, various years)

Table 3 **Japan's defence expenditure 1975–2004 calculated in yen and US dollars, and as a percentage of GNP and annual government expenditure**				
Year	Yen millions	US$ millions	% GNP	% annual govt exp.
1975	1,327.3	4,484	0.84	6.23
1976	1,512.4	5,058	0.90	6.22
1977	1,690.6	6,100	0.88	5.93
1978	1,901.0	8,570	0.90	5.54
1979	2,094.5	10,080	0.90	5.43
1980	2,230.2	8,960	0.90	5.24
1981	2,400.0	11,500	0.91	5.24
1982	2,586.1	10,360	0.93	5.21
1983	2,754.2	11,617	0.98	5.47
1984	2,934.6	12,018	0.99	5.80
1985	3,137.1	14,189	1.00	5.98
1986	3,343.5	20,930	0.93	6.18
1987	3,517.4	25,420	1.00	6.50
1988	3,700.3	28,850	1.01	6.53
1989	3,919.8	30,090	1.01	6.49
1990	4,159.3	28,122	1.00	6.28
1991	4,386.0	32,890	0.95	6.23
1992	4,551.8	34,300	0.94	6.30
1993	4,640.6	39,710	0.94	6.41
1994	4,683.5	42,100	0.96	6.41
1995	4,723.6	53,800	0.96	6.65
1996	4,845.5	45,100	0.98	6.45
1997	4,941.4	42,900	0.96	6.39
1998	4,929.0	35,200	0.95	6.35
1999	4,920.1	41,100	0.99	6.01
2000	4,921.8	45,600	0.99	5.79
2001	4,938.8	40,400	0.95	5.98
2002	4,939.5	39,500	1.00	6.08
2003	4,926.5	41,600	0.99	6.02
2004	4,876.4	45,151	0.97	5.94

Source: Asagumo Shimbunsha, *Boei Handobukku* (Tokyo: Asagumo Shimbunsha, various years); International Institute for Strategic Studies, *The Military Balance* (Oxford: Oxford University Press, relevant years).

ceiling on defence expenditure. Moreover, the procurement element of the budget for arms and equipment has moved in line with the overall defence budget by stagnating and slightly decreasing, set at around ¥0.9 trillion over the last decade. The defence budget's share of the total government expenditure has remained stable at around 6%; and, despite the intermittent breaching of the principle under the Nakasone administration in the mid- to late-1980s, has remained below 1% of GNP. The stagnation of Japan's defence budget contrasts with that of other non-European states, many of which have increased military expenditure since the end of the 1990s (most notably the US and China). Japan's military expenditure per capita still remains lower than that of US, UK, Germany and France.[9] Finally, the size of Japan's defence budget and its purchasing power for weaponry needs to be moderated by the fact that high personnel costs account for around 45% of the total budget, and procurement only around 19%.

Thus, Japan still has massive potential, if necessary, to increase its military spending to match its economic size. Now that its economy is growing once more, it may be able to increase spending even within the 1% of GNP. But Japan's severe general government budget constraints at present, and continued constitutional restrictions, mean that the government faces tough choices over the prioritisation of the acquisition of certain capabilities. Between 1996 and 2003, the GSDF's tank force was reduced from 1,110 to just over 1,000; MSDF destroyers were reduced from 58 to 54, and ASDF fighters from 431 to 363, all representing cuts of around 10% or more, with further cuts planned for the new revised NDPO.[10] Nevertheless,

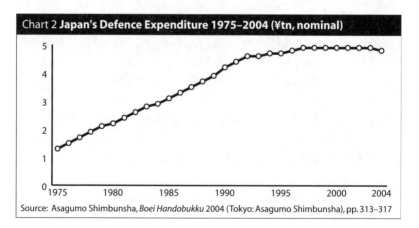

Chart 2 **Japan's Defence Expenditure 1975–2004 (¥tn, nominal)**

Source: Asagumo Shimbunsha, *Boei Handobukku* 2004 (Tokyo: Asagumo Shimbunsha), pp. 313–317

Japan has so far managed to maintain and procure a range of high-tech capabilities and very significant military firepower. Tables 4, 5, and 6 illustrate the current JSDF strength. Japanese policymakers remain confident that there is sufficient budgetary flexibility to acquire highly expensive items such as BMD and the others listed below. Japan's procurement budget for equipment is static, but its practice of deferring payments ('saimu futan koi') for major acquisitions over a five-year period, and the relatively long lead-in time of programmes such as BMD, enable it to string out and manage the costs over the longer term.[11]

JSDF qualitative build-up: new power-projection capabilities

Japan has produced three Mid-Term Defence Programmes (MTDP) ('Chuki Boeiryokyu Seibi Keikaku') since the end of the Cold War, covering the periods 1991–95, 1996–2000 and 2001–05. These bring JSDF strengths into line with the NDPO targets and incorporate plans for the qualitative upgrading of capabilities. Under the MTDP, the GSDF has acquired the highly sophisticated M-90 main battle tank; the AH-1S and anti-tank and ground-attack helicopter; the UH-60JA multi-role helicopter; and the upgraded *Hawk* surface-to-air missile. The GSDF has acquired funding to improve its equipment to deal with guerrilla incursions and nuclear, chemical and biological warfare. In March 2004, the GSDF established a 300-member special operations unit, mainly consisting of elite airborne troops, to assist the police in the gathering of intelligence on, tracking and arrest of suspected terrorists – once again intruding on traditional policing duties and using this new arena of activity to establish a new legitimacy for itself.[12]

The MSDF has plans to increase its number of *Aegis* war-fighting system (AWS) *Kongo*-class destroyers, the essential platforms for Japan's introduction of a BMD system, from four to six. Japan's coastal protection against 'fushinsen' and other intruder vessels has been beefed up by procuring 200-tonne high-speed missile patrol boats, and the JCG's installation of 30mm long-range machine guns on its ships. The MSDF also aims to acquire a total of three *Osumi*-class transport ships. These ships have flat-topped decks that enable the landing of helicopter transports, plus an integral rear dock for the operation of hovercraft capable of landing tanks on shore. The MSDF

Table 4 **GSDF Armoured vehicles and Artillery in 2003**	
Type	**Number**
Main battle tanks	1,030
Armoured personnel carriers	830
Field artillery	750
Recoilless guns	3,190
Rocket launchers	1,700
Mortars	1,880
Anti-aircraft machine guns	110

Source: Boeichohen, *Boei Hakusho 2003* (Tokyo: Zaimusho Insatsukyoku, 2003), pp. 336–338; Asagumo Shimbunsha, *Jieitai Sobi Nenkan 2003–2004* (Tokyo: Asagumo Shimbunsha, 2004), pp. 58–77; Asagumo Shimbunsha, *Boei Handobukku* (Tokyo: Asagumo Shimbunhsa, 2004), pp. 322; International Institute for Strategic Studies, *The Military Balance* 2003/4 (Oxford: Oxford University Press, 2003), pp. 158–159.

Table 5 **MSDF Major Combatant Ships in 2003**	
Type	**Number of Vessels**
DESTROYERS	**54**
Destroyers	43
Destroyer Escorts	9
SUBMARINES	**16**
MINE WARFARE SHIPS	**31**
Minesweeper Ocean	3
Minesweeper Coastal	24
Minesweeper Tender	2
Minesweeping Controller	2
MISSILE-ARMED PATROL CRAFT	**7**
AMPHIBIOUS SHIPS	**8**
Landing Ship Tank	4
Landing Ship Utility	2
Landing Craft Utility	2
AUXILLARY AND SUPPORT SHIPS	
(combat support ships, service ships, rescue ships, icebreaker)	26

Source: Boeichohen, *Boei Hakusho 2003* (Tokyo: Zaimusho Insatsukyoku, 2003), pp. 336–338; Asagumo Shimbunsha, *Jieitai Sobi Nenkan 2003-2004* (Tokyo: Asagumo Shimbunsha, 2004), pp. 217–218; Asagumo Shimbunsha, *Boei Handobukku 2004* (Tokyo: Asagumo Shimbunhsa, 2004), p. 323; International Institute for Strategic Studies, *The Military Balance* 2003/4 (Oxford: Oxford University Press, 2003), pp. 158–159.

Table 6 **ASDF, GSDF and MSDF Major Aircraft in 2003**				
Service	**Model Type**	**Function**	**Model**	**Number**
ASDF	Fixed-wing	Combat	F-15J/DJ	203
			F-4EJ	92
			F-1	25
			F-2A/B	40
		Reconnaissance	RF-4E/EJ	27
		Early-warning	E-2C	13
		Early-warning and control	E-767	4
		Transport	C-1	26
			C-130H	16
	Helicopter	Transport	CH-47J	17
GSDF	Fixed-wing	Liaison and Reconnaissance	LR-1, LR-2	16
	Helicopter	Anti-tank	AH-1S	89
		Observation	OH-6D	162
			OH-1	16
		Transport	V-107A	1
			CH-47J/JA	49
		Utility	UH-1H/J	157
			UH-60JA	21
MSDF	Fixed-wing	Patrol/ASW	P-3C	99
	Helicopter	Patrol/ASW	HSS-2B	6
			SH-60J	91
		Minesweeping and transport	MH-53E	10

Source: Boeichohen, *Boei Hakusho 2004* (Tokyo: Zaimusho Insatsukyoku, 2004), pp. 332–336; Asagumo Shimbunsha, *Jieitai Sobi Nenkan 2003–2004* (Tokyo: Asagumo Shimbunsha, 2004), pp. 392; Asagumo Shimbunsha, *Boei Handobukku* (Tokyo: Asagumo Shimbunhsa, 2003), pp. 313–323; International Institute for Strategic Studies, *The Military Balance* 2003/4 (Oxford: Oxford University Press, 2003), pp. 158–159.

justifies these ships as being necessary for the transport of the GSDF to UN PKO and for other operations in support of international peace. The first *Osumi*-class vessel was deployed to East Timor in 1999 and to Iraq in 2003. The flat top of the *Osumi*-class and its side-positioned super-structure has aroused suspicion that it is the first step in constructing a vertical/short takeoff and landing (VSTOL) aircraft carrier; however, the thinness of the decks on the *Osumi*-class effectively rules this out.

Similarly, the MSDF has plans to construct up to four new class DDH (Destroyer–Helicopter) destroyers, each carrying four helicopters. The original rationale for the DDH destroyers was ASW, but more recently, the MSDF has argued that they serve a similar transport function to the *Osumi*-class, as well for the evacuation of Japanese nationals in a natural disaster or from overseas during a conflict.[13] Early official MSDF and JDA sketches for the DDH show a centrally mounted superstructure and integral hangars, separating large flight decks forward and aft, in a more traditional destroyer configuration. However, later JDA official plans show a starboard-positioned island superstructure with a continuous flight deck fore and aft, and an aircraft lift. Presumably the DDH will have below-deck hangars.[14] This has again raised speculation that Japan is intent on acquiring VSTOL aircraft carriers, which at 13,500 tonnes in displacement would make them larger than Thailand's *Chakri Nareubet* carrier, and possibly capable of carrying a maritime version of the F-35 Joint Strike Fighter. The probability is that the weakness of the decks (as with the *Osumi*-class transports) would rule out an aircraft-carrier type role. Nevertheless, the configuration of the *Osumi* and DDH-class indicates that Japan is rehearsing carrier-building technology to reserve for itself this potential military option; and thus, that it is considering discarding the constitutional prohibition on the acquisition of power-projection capacities. The MSDF also plans to develop an indigenously manufactured replacement, P-X, for its P-3C early-warning aircraft (although it may reconsider this position to introduce the US Multimission Maritime Aircraft to save costs and enhance interoperability with the US).

The ASDF's intentions are as follows: to upgrade the radar and avionics of its F-15s; to continue with the introduction of the F-2 fighter co-developed with the US; and to develop a C-X transport aircraft to replace the C-1. Looking towards the MTDP of 2005–09, the ADSF is also believed to be considering acquisition of F-35 Joint Strike Fighters to replace the aging F-4EJs.[15] The ASDF has acquired a role in BMD through upgrading 24 *Patriot* Advanced Capability-2 (PAC-2) batteries to act as a PAC-3 missile interceptor system. Most significantly, the ASDF is set to procure, after prolonged lobbying, four Boeing-767 tanker aircraft and an in-flight refuelling capability (and the ASDF may try to double this number of tanker aircraft in the 2005–9 MTDP). The ASDF argues that this is necessary to extend the range of its transports engaged in UN PKO and other international cooperation missions; to prolong the time that its fighters can remain airborne and thus make more efficient use of pilot time in the air and fuel for takeoff and landing, as well as thereby reducing the noise from frequent takeoffs and landings; and to allow aircraft to remain in the air when poor weather conditions prevents safe landing.[16] However, in-flight refuelling clearly provides the ASDF with a new power-projection capacity to fly sorties across East Asia and beyond. Consequently, speculation has arisen among Japan's neighbours that Tokyo might use this capability to launch preemptive strikes against North Korean ballistic missiles, although – as later sections of this paper will argue – this speculation is largely unfounded. Still, at the very least, the acquisition of in-flight refuelling capability is a further demonstration, as in the case of the MSDF's experimentation with carrier technology, that Japan is testing constitutional restrictions on power-projection.

Japan and the RMA

The JSDF has acknowledged the need to improve its capabilities to keep in step with the changes in military strategy heralded by the RMA. Japan views this as essential for two reasons: firstly, in an era of stagnant defence budgets, to maintain a lead over potential regional rivals through technological and qualitative rather than quantitative means; and, secondly, to maintain a force structure capable of interoperability with the ever-more sophisticated military of its US ally.

Japan's primary efforts in the RMA to date have concentrated on the upgrading of its Battle Management Command, Control, Computers and Intelligence (BMC4I) systems. The JSDF's three services have employed three different command-and-control systems (GSDF Ground Self Defence Force Network [G-NET]; MSDF Maritime Operational Fleet [MOF]; and ASDF Base Air Defence Ground Environment [BADGE]). The existence of these distinct BMC4I systems has complicated data-linking and operational coordination within the JSDF and hampered its ability to respond in real time to military contingencies. Additionally, they prevent full interoperability with the US in conventional operations and in the context of BMD architectures, which demand rapid data exchange between Japanese and US command-and-control systems. This is a particular problem for the GSDF and ASDF, which, in contrast to the MSDF, do not possess BMC4I software and hardware refined to enhance communication with the US. Consequently, under the most recent MTDP, Japan has sought to upgrade the BADGE system as the prime coordinator of Japanese air defence for a BMD system. Japan plans also to create a network to enable information sharing among the three JSDF command-and-control systems in the form of a Common Operating Environment (COE) and Defence Information Infrastructure (DII). In 2003, the JDA established a Central Command and Control System (CCS) connected to the three JSDF BMC4I systems, which ensures more comprehensive command and control over military operations from the centre.[17]

The JDA has taken steps to protect its information systems from the risks of cyber-terrorism – a form of asymmetric warfare that could conceivably be practiced by states such as China and North Korea. Japan's potential vulnerability was demonstrated by a series of hacker attacks in January and February 2000 that succeeded in defacing government web sites. The NPA reported more than 51,000 attempted cyber-incursions into police computer systems between July and September 2002.[18] The JDA has engaged in long-term research to harden its own systems against the cyber threat.

In the next stage of its response to the RMA, the JSDF has embarked upon a programme of organisational change and force integration to facilitate joint operations. The current decision-making structure for joint operations within the JSDF consists of the JSC and the three service chiefs of staff. The JDA notes that this has not proved conducive to joint operations, as the JSC functions more in an advisory than command role in executing the JDA Director General's policy. Each Chief of Staff individually advises the Director General and carries out his orders – in practice, this means that each service acts separately in accordance with its own doctrine.[19] Japanese defence plans now call for the institution of a new Joint Staff Organisation (JSO). The Chief of the JSO, drawn from one of the services, will represent all three services, and become both the principal military advisor to the Director General and the principal military conduit for relaying civilian orders to the JSDF. This system appears to be modelled on that of the US. In July 2004, the current MSDF Chief of Staff, Koichi Furusho, proposed that the newly appointed Chief of the Staff of the JSO should not be under the control of JDA bureaucrats.[20] The authority of the JSO vis-à-vis the JDA internal bureaux is yet to be clarified, but the new position should enable smoother coordination between senior political civilian and military commanders, greater JSDF force integration, and enhance interoperability with the US.

Japan is also intent on inquiring the type of sophisticated weaponry employed by the US that complements and is leveraged in its effectiveness by more flexible force integration and command and control. The JSDF may have interest in acquiring Unmanned Aerial Vehicles (UAV); in March 2004, the JDA was reported to have decided to procure precision-guided bombs, or Joint Direct Attack Munitions (JDAM), from the US. NDPO planners are rumoured to have considered the value of acquiring *Tomahawk* missiles for the MSDF.[21] It remains to be seen if this informational, organisational and capability-related response to the RMA brings about doctrinal change in Japan's defence posture.

Japan's intelligence capabilities and satellite programme

Japan has sought to develop an extensive array of intelligence capabilities. The NPA and Tokyo Metropolitan Police Department (MPD) security bureaux and the Ministry of Justice's Public Security Investigation Agency (PSIA) gather intelligence on domestic and international radical and terrorist groups. MOFA has an Information and Analysis Bureau, and each of the JSDF services has an intelligence arm.[22]

In 1997, the JDA established the Japan Defence Intelligence Headquarters (JDIH), in an attempt to integrate JSDF intelligence-gathering assets, the JDA's First and Second Research Divisions, and JSC's Second Staff Office. The JDIH is under the JSC and is controlled by the Defence Intelligence Committee (DIC) consisting of the

Administrative Vice-Minister, the Director of the Defence Bureau, the Chairman of the JSC and the three JSDF chiefs of staff. Interestingly, the Director of the JDIH is a uniformed officer and the Deputy Director a JDA bureaucrat, marking the first time that military personnel have been ranked above civilians in the JDA and the further 'normalisation' of the JSDF role.[23] The JDIH has a total staff of 1,800 JSDF personnel and civilians, and is divided into six sections: General Affairs, Planning, Analysis, Imagery, Emergency Response and Signals Intelligence (SIGINT). The SIGINT Division is the largest, with 1,300 personnel, giving the JDIH the character of the US National Security Agency.

Japan's intelligence community is under the overall direction of the Cabinet Secretariat's Cabinet Information Research Office (CIRO) ('Naikaku Joho Chosashitsu'). However, the coordination of these various intelligence capabilities remains a crucial problem for Japanese security policymakers. Japanese intelligence has been undercut in the past by the vertical inter-jurisdictional conflicts among ministries. The 1995 revised NDPO stressed the need for Japan to improve its capabilities and the JDIH was one outcome. Nevertheless, the JDIH has, in certain ways, enhanced inter-ministerial rivalries, with the NPA, MOFA and elements of Japanese political leadership concerned that the JDA and JSDF may use their elevated position in intelligence gathering to increase their influence over the Kantei. The CIRO is charged with formal responsibility in a Central Intelligence Agency-type fashion for coordinating Japan's intelligence, but it lacks manpower, having only 130 permanent officials of its own, and 179 other officials drawn from competing ministries.

In addition to Japan's efforts to enhance information-sharing, it has sought to enhance its overall intelligence-gathering capacity through the development of its own spy satellites. Japan's interest in an independent satellite capability has been spurred on by North Korean ballistic missile tests since 1994, especially the 'Taepo-dong shock' of August 1998. The JDA has been in receipt of US satellite intelligence about missile launches via links from the US National Reconnaissance Office and US Forces Headquarters in Japan at Yokota. Forewarned about the *Taepo-dong*-1 launch, Japan deployed AWS-equipped destroyers and EP-3 early-warning aircraft to the Sea of Japan and was able to detect the actual missile launch by their radar.[24] Japan's radar capabilities, though, were not sufficient to detect the final trajectory of the missile: it was reliant upon US satellites for this information. The US duly passed this information to the JDA; however, the fact of Japan being informed in this way by the US was not made readily available to policymakers outside the central executive, or to the media. There are a variety of possible reasons for this, including technical difficulties in Japan–US information-sharing, organisational inertia, or even a political conspiracy on the Japanese or US sides to suppress this information to heighten the sense of Japan's vulnerability to missiles and generate support for military cooperation against the North Korea. The result was strong dissatisfaction among elements of the LDP regarding Japan's over-dependence on US satellite information and a corresponding determination to push for the acquisition of an independent, indigenously produced capability; a move backed by civilian defence contractors eager to secure new procurement orders for the satellites.[25]

From 1998 onwards, the Japanese government decided to deploy four satellites, two optical and two with synthetic aperture radar (SAR). These were classified as multi-purpose 'information-gathering satellites', which could be used not only for military purposes, but also to monitor weather patterns, natural disasters and smuggling. The obfuscation of the primary purpose of the satellites was to enable Japan to circumvent its 1969 prohibition on the use of space for military purposes. The Japanese government hopes that these satellites, while not able to detect the actual event of a missile launch (a capability only provided by infra-red sensor US satellites), will be able to detect changes in deployments of military assets and preparation for a missile launch and thus enable Japan to ready its diplomatic or military response. Japan used these satellites with some success in September 2004 to monitor North Korea's potential preparations for a missile launch, as well as in April of the same year to confirm that a blast at Ryongchon near the North's border with China was in fact a train explosion. To process the information from the satellites, Japan has established a Cabinet Satellite Intelligence Centre (CSIC) under the CIRO, with a staff of around 320, including 100 analysts.

Japan's satellite programme has encountered criticism and difficulties. The US was initially opposed, seeing the programme as an unnecessary, expensive (the total cost is estimated at ¥250bn) and less-capable duplication of satellite information already available to

Japan through the bilateral alliance. The US preferred a model of a joint intelligence centre, to strengthen alliance cooperation, but eventually relented, so as not to strain alliance relations. The US criticisms are partly valid: Japan's satellites are likely to have a resolution of only one metre, which simply matches commercially available imagery, and will never match the 15cm resolution provided by US military satellites.[26] In any case, Japan will have to rely on US training for its analysts and the supply of certain key components in the satellites. Finally, despite Japan's initial success in launching two satellites in March 2003, the programme encountered a major blow in November of same year when the H-IIA rocket to carry two more satellites in orbit was destroyed on its launch.

Nevertheless, despite the shortcomings and setbacks, the satellite programme, coupled with the JDIH, is significant in that it sets Japan on the path towards greater information-gathering capabilities that, in the long term may rival those of the US, strengthen its overall military position in the region and raise its standing within the bilateral alliance.

Challenging post-war security taboos and constitutional restraints

Pre-emptive strikes?

Many domestic and foreign observers have expressed concern that Japan's acquisition of an in-flight refuelling capability will lead it not only to breach its ban on power-projection capabilities, but also towards the exercise of pre-emptive strikes. The Japanese government has hinted at its willingness to take direct military action against North Korean missiles. For instance, on 3 March 1999, then-JDA Director General Hosei Norota, in response to a question in the House of Representatives Standing Committee on Security, argued that Japan could launch defensive air strikes against North Korean missile sites without contravening constitutional prohibitions. In January 2003, then JDA Director General Shigeru Ishiba restated Japan's right to strike North Korean missile bases, at the height of international concerns about North Korea's withdrawal from the NPT. The comments of Norota and Ishiba were taken by sections of both the Japanese and foreign media to represent a new government stance permitting pre-emptive strikes and an obvious warning to North Korea against another missile test.

Since 1999, however, the JDA has argued consistently that this speculation is a misinterpretation of Japan's stance regarding attacks on bases overseas and that pre-emptive strikes are not permissible. The original Japanese government position on this issue was formulated in a pronouncement in the House of Representatives in 1956. This stated that, in the event 'sudden and unjust harm' ('kinpaku fusei no higai') is inflicted upon Japan by means of a guided missile, then Japan, in line with the purport of the constitution – which does not mandate total passivity in the face of destruction – is permitted within the bounds of self-defence to launch an attack on the missile bases, using the most moderate degree of force possible, and only if there is no alternative.[27] However, under Japanese government definitions, pre-emptive strikes are not permitted: 'sudden and unjust harm' is judged to occur only when an aggressor country has actually taken concrete steps to embark upon an action that would inflict damage. But mere fears that an aggressor country is about to take these steps are insufficient grounds for Japan to launch an attack in self-defence.

Norota's comments in the National Diet in March 1999 did not go beyond simply stating that, 'it is legally possible for Japan to attack enemy bases, even at a point of time when no damage has actually been inflicted upon Japan'. Norota left moot the point as to whether he was referring to attacks in response to an instance of when an aggressor country had actually embarked upon an action which would imminently inflict damage on Japan – which meets the criteria of the definition of 'sudden and unjust harm' and would thus be permissible – or to attacks when an aggressor country was feared to be about to embark upon an action that would imminently inflict damage upon Japan – which comes under the definition of a pre-emptive strike and is thus non-permissible under the 1956 ruling. Norota's non-specification of the second set of conditions means that his statement cannot be taken to represent a new Japanese government interpretation regarding the constitutionality of pre-emptive strikes.[28] Similarly, Ishiba's remarks in 2003 were prefaced by, and did not stray from, the 1956 definition of a non-pre-emptive strikes against missile bases, and thus represented no change in the Japanese position. During questioning in the Diet, however, Ishiba was pushed to provide some cautious elaboration of the conditions that would be judged to mark the start of steps to actually inflict damage.

He indicated that these steps would be connected to clear pronouncements from a state such as North Korea that it would launch an attack and the observed fuelling of missiles.[29]

Japan's arms export ban lifted?

Since 1976, Japan has maintained a total ban on exports of arms and military technology, with the exception of a partial breach of the ban in 1983 to enable US–Japan technological cooperation on the Star Wars programme and the Fighter Support Experimental (FS-X; now in service as the F-2). There were also inadvertent breaches through the export of essentially civilian but dual-use technologies, such as maritime radars, transport trucks, and patrol boats, that have been utilised for military purposes.[30] In recent years, however, the Japanese government has increasingly indicated that it will seek further partial breaches, or even the general abandonment, of the arms export ban principle.

The first reason, and the point of departure for further breaches, is Japan's decision to jointly develop with the US a BMD system that will require a higher volume of two-way technology sharing and transfer. Secondly, Japan's defence planners see the removal of the ban on military technology transfer as necessary to entering into joint projects with the US and third countries that can produce interoperable defence equipment for participation in multinational peace and security activities.

Third is the concern that Japan's domestic armaments industry, as a result of the export ban, is falling behind other advanced industrial states or potential regional military competitors. In the post-war period, Japan has built up, through a policy of indigenous production ('kokusanka') a sophisticated military industrial base, with world-class strengths in sensors and elements of missile technology.[31] The JDA's Technology Research and Development Institute (TRDI) is responsible for the development of certain military technologies; however, the bulk of Japan's military production base is located within the defence arms of large civilian conglomerates, such as Mitsubishi Heavy Industries, Kawasaki Heavy Industries, Ishikawajima-Harima Heavy Industries and Fuji Heavy Industries. For these corporations, in contrast to many US prime defence contractors, defence production represents a small percentage of their overall turnover (no more than 10.5%), and they rely on process of developing dual-use civilian technologies that can then, in a process of 'spin-on', be utilised for military purposes.[32] Japan is known, though, to be weak in key areas of technology such as systems integration, and is reliant on the US for licensed production technology or for joint production, as in the case of the FS-X. The military export ban is perceived as compounding these weaknesses. Japanese defence producers' reliance on JSDF as their sole customer and the absence of an export market means that, although they have a guaranteed customer, they cannot enjoy economies of scale. For instance, Japan's M-90 tank, produced in low volume to sustain a 'hot' production base for emergency use, turns out a unit at a cost of US$7–9 million, compared to US$2.2m for a US M-1 tank, thereby making the M-90 the most expensive tank in the world.[33] The consequences are spiralling production costs, greater strain on an already tight defence budget, and therefore, declining orders and profits. In addition, the inability of Japanese defence contractors to form alliances and mergers with overseas contractors, as do European and US contractors, denies them another avenue to exploit economies of scale and to leverage new forms of technology. The potential outcome is the reduction in incentives for civilian conglomerates to invest in defence production and leading-edge technologies. In turn, the erosion of Japan's technological capabilities may lead to ever greater dependency on imported technologies, particularly from the US, and the further undermining of 'kokusanka' and Japanese defence autonomy. Japan's big-ticket procurement programmes for BMD, satellites and in the MTDP offer some relief for Japan's defence producers; although the initial procurement of BMD is likely to be based on 'black-boxed' technology from the US, thereby serving to accentuate Japanese technological dependency within the alliance. Moreover, despite the expressed wish of the JDA since September 2004 to continue and expand joint development of BMD with the US to include sensor and control systems, the exact status and continuation of the joint programme and the US's willingness to share non-black boxed technology with Japan may be in some doubt.

Increasingly, Japan's policymakers see an end to the exports ban as the key to reversing the decline in the domestic defence production base and preserving a degree of 'kokusanka' through international cooperation. In January 2004, then JDA Director General Ishiba, in a speech in the Hague, touched upon the need to lift the ban on exports to facilitate defence production with the US and other countries. In reaction to Ishiba's bold comments, the Kantei later stressed that the government was considering a further partial lifting only with regard to the US and BMD. Nevertheless, Ishiba's comments did reflect strengthening opinion within the JDA, the JSDF and segments of domestic industry regarding the need to end the export bans. Moreover, as noted in Chapter 2, the LDP's Defence Policy Subcommittee in 2004 proposed that the total ban be lifted in favour of an export licensing scheme. This call was repeated by the Keidanren, the principal business association in Japan, in July of the same year. Abe Shinzo has advocated a return to the principles of the 1967 ban on arms exports to communist countries, countries under UN sanctions and states party to conflict, thereby clearing the way for high-tech weapons sales and co-production with other developed states.[34] The Prime Minister's Council on Security and Defence Capabilities commented that expanding technological military cooperation with states other than the US should not be seen as Japan acting as a 'merchant of death'.[35] Even though the ban on exports remains in place, the pressure for its total breach in the near future is becoming relentless.

Japan's nuclear option?

Japan's potential to 'go nuclear' has been a perennial debate domestically and internationally. If Japan were to exercise this option, this would clearly mark the most dramatic turning point in its post-war security policy. As pointed out in Chapter 1, since 1958 Japan has publicly maintained that it is constitutionally entitled to possess nuclear weapons for the exclusive purpose of self-defence. An additional restraint on Japan's potential exercise of a nuclear option was created by Prime Minister Sato's 1967 introduction of the three non-nuclear principles, for which he received the Nobel Peace Prize in 1974. Sato's receipt of the prize is perhaps ironic, given that he was motivated more by political expediency than genuine anti-nuclearism: he enunciated the anti-nuclear principles as a means to mute the opposition from the Left on security policy, but then still concluded a secret agreement with the US to allow the entry of nuclear weapons into Japanese ports on naval ships. Moreover, in spite of the three non-nuclear principles, Japan's policymakers have continued to study the viability of a nuclear option. Sato himself initiated secret and unofficial CIRO studies in 1968 and 1970 on the desirability and feasibility of Japan's acquisition of nuclear weapons; in 1995 the JDA compiled a similar report for internal use, entitled *A Report Concerning the Problems of Proliferation of Weapons of Mass Destruction*. Importantly, though, both reports concluded that Japan's development of nuclear weapons was not a credible security option as long as it could rely on the US extended nuclear umbrella, and that the domestic political, technological and international diplomatic costs of Japan's going nuclear were too great.[36]

In recent years, speculation about Japan's interest in a nuclear option has been driven by a combination of the stockpiling, from its civilian nuclear programme, of plutonium that is believed to have weapons applicability; Japan's resistance to the indefinite extension of the NPT in 1993; and its undoubted overall technological potential to develop nuclear weapons.[37] Statements by Japanese politicians on nuclear issues, set against the background of concerns about North Korea's nuclear programme, and an upgrading of China's nuclear capabilities, have also been taken as signs of a shift in the non-nuclear stance. In October 1999, Shingo Nishimura, the parliamentary vice-minister of the JDA, was dismissed for suggesting Japan's failure to consider the acquisition of nuclear weapons left the country vulnerable to 'rape'. In April 2002, Ichiro Ozawa reported that, during a recent trip to Beijing, he had told Chinese leaders, 'If Japan desires, it can possess thousands of nuclear warheads. Japan has enough plutonium in use at its nuclear power plants for three to four thousand … If that should happen, we wouldn't lose [to China] in terms of military strength'.[38] Speculation was further fuelled in May and June 2002 when, in response to direct questions on the issue, Shinzo Abe and Yasuo Fukuda restated the government's consistent policy line that possession of nuclear weapons was constitutional. Since the North Korean crisis of 1994, US policymakers have often expressed concerns that North Korea's acquisition of nuclear weapons would push Japan towards its own nuclear option.[39]

Undoubtedly, Japan has the constitutional flexibility to acquire an independent nuclear deterrent. Its policymakers continue to study this option, and recent debates in Japan on nuclear weapons demonstrate that the issue is increasingly less of a policy taboo. Nevertheless, the conclusion of most policymakers and analysts is that over the short to medium term, Japan has no real strategic interest in acquiring nuclear weapons and would face considerable technological obstacles in building them. In June 2002, Prime Minister Koizumi confirmed that Japan was 'never going to change its non-nuclear policy'.[40]

The reasons for Japan's lack of interest in acquiring nuclear weapons have not essentially changed. Despite the potential threat from North Korean nuclear weapons and the upgrading of China's nuclear force, Japan continues to have confidence in the US nuclear umbrella as providing a sufficient deterrent guarantee against these states. In addition, Japan's acquisition of a BMD system is seen as a means to potentially counter North Korea's nuclear threat without resorting to its own nuclear deterrent. Japan's policymakers are also aware that Japan's acquisition of nuclear weapons might provoke a destabilising and counterproductive nuclear arms race in the region, endanger ties with the US and undermine Japan's international reputation as a responsible non-nuclear power.

In addition, despite its technological prowess, Japan does face considerable technological hurdles in nuclear weapons development. Japanese plutonium stockpiles might be suitable for the creation of nuclear warheads, but this could only be carried out with great expense and difficulty.[41] Moreover, Japan's strict adherence to NPT safeguards means that it cannot conduct a clandestine programme; it would need openly to declare a military nuclear option and endure all the international pressure that this entails. Furthermore, Japan has no experience of nuclear testing and no suitable delivery systems. Japan has no long-range bombers; its HII civilian rocket is liquid-fuelled and unsuited to functioning as a ballistic missile. Japan's tight geographical confines mean that any land-based nuclear deterrent in fixed silos would be easily targeted by enemy first strikes. Japan would need to develop a submarine-based deterrent, but it has no nuclear-powered ship technologies. Finally, Japan at present lacks technology for inertial missile guidance and re-entry systems, adequate satellite communication networks and BMC4I capabilities.[42] These difficulties could probably be overcome in the longer term, but an indigenous nuclear deterrent would still be no ready replacement for that of the US.

Japan's nuclear option, therefore, is unlikely to become a reality in the immediate future. Its policymakers remain convinced of the benefits of the US nuclear umbrella, and wary of the technological problems of creating an independent deterrent. Japan is likely to remain as a 'threshold' or recessed nuclear power, and to retain the threat of the option of going nuclear, a position that affords it greater leverage vis-à-vis the US and its neighbours. Japan's principal energies on nuclear issues will be devoted instead to initiatives for nuclear disarmament. Indeed, Japan's opposition in 1993 to indefinite NPT renewal should be explained not as a desire to retain a nuclear option for itself, but to exert some influence on the existing nuclear powers to follow their own pledges under Article 6 of the treaty to cut their arsenals. But even if Japan remains a non-nuclear power itself and practices a form of 'unilateral arms control', its advocacy of nuclear disarmament will not be without contradictions. Japan's preaching of nuclear disarmament and non-proliferation for others, while relying on the biggest nuclear power in the world for protection, is highly incongruous.

Conclusion

Japan is set to acquire many of the capabilities of a 'normal' advanced military power. The JSDF, even within an increasingly constrained military budget, has embarked on a fundamental qualitative upgrading of its military capabilities, including, most notably, actual and latent power-projection capabilities, complemented by new RMA and intelligence capabilities. Japan has also shown, through the passing of new emergency legislation, that it is serious about the need for war-fighting preparedness. In addition, traditional constitutional prohibitions on pre-emptive strikes, arms exports and nuclear weapons are increasingly under question and close to being breached, or have ceased at least to be taboo subjects for debate.

The Japanese military has the size and sophistication to pack a potential punch in conventional terms second only to that of the US in the Asia–Pacific, and exceeds the capabilities of developed states in other regions. Nevertheless, Japan's build-up of military capabilities does not indicate that it seeks as yet to depart from an exclusively defence-oriented policy, or that it is moving towards a more independent security role. Japan's new capabilities are, in part, designed to reinforce its role in UN-led international security activities. Even more importantly, though, the JSDF's strengthened capabilities are designed to work in concert with the capabilities of the US. Japan's NDPO makes clear the deepening linkages between

Japan's defence doctrine and bilateral cooperation with the US: the JSDF force structure is becoming ever more skewed to the point that Japan cannot defend itself without US assistance. Japan's new power-projection capabilities are designed not for an autonomous defence role, but to reinforce the JSDF's ability to take part in expeditionary warfare and US-led coalitions, as in Afghanistan and Iraq. Hence, even though Japan has acquired some greater degree of potential autonomy and hedging options in defence – as in the case of satellite information – on the whole, its national defence build-up is an alliance-oriented defence build-up.

In the overall trajectory of Japan's post-Cold War security policy, Japan is retaining part of the Yoshida doctrine through staying close to the US, but jettisoning key parts that stressed the need, eventually, for a more autonomous defence posture that would provide Japan with the option of hedging against dependence on the US. The next chapter will examine Japan's increasing dependence on the bilateral alliance for determining the future trajectory of its security policy.

Chapter 4

Forging a strengthened US–Japan alliance

Rescuing the alliance

In the early post-Cold War period, Japan and the US soon discovered that, despite the efforts of the past 40 years to strengthen bilateral military cooperation, they shared a security treaty that was largely still masquerading as an alliance. Under the strategic bargain forged during the Cold War, Japan was very much the junior partner, acquiescing in reliance upon the US for military security. The US was content to take on the responsibility of Japan's defence under this arrangement, because this allowed the US access to bases that were vital for power projection and the containment of communism in East Asia. Japan's main concern in the treaty was Article 5 and the immediate defence of Japan; for the US, the key concern was Article 6 and response to regional contingencies. As the Cold War progressed, Japan and the US developed a military division of labour, and by the 1980s, the security treaty began to take on the trappings of an 'alliance'. Japan acquired defence capabilities to complement and provide a 'shield' for US forces based in Japan, which would act as the 'sword' for regional power projection against the USSR. Japan's constitutional restrictions and its ongoing concerns about entrapment in US regional strategy prevented full commitment to military cooperation with the US. Nevertheless, the strategic bargain, with its asymmetric division of labour, was able to function during the Cold War, thanks to the overlap of Japanese and American strategic interests: the common Soviet threat blurred the distinction between Japan's activities under the security treaty to provide for its own defence and those activities providing support for the US that could have been construed as providing for the defence of the US and East Asia region in a collective self-defence fashion.

In the post-Cold War period, this strategic bargain threatened to come unstuck as a series of global and regional crises revealed its essential emptiness, as already explained in Chapter 2. In the early 1990s, Japan and the US faced the very real prospect that their efforts to construct a genuine alliance were unravelling – a concern most especially revealed by the alliance's abject failure to respond to the first North Korean nuclear crisis. Since then, however, policymakers in both countries have concluded that the bilateral alliance is indispensable to their respective security interests. The US, for its part, views the alliance as the linchpin of its bilateral alliance system and its presence in the region, and thus has sought to preserve it – although making clear its desire for the alliance to be re-strengthened by reducing the asymmetries in military cooperation and by orienting it towards responding to Article 6-type contingencies. Japan, for its part sees the alliance as crucial for inter-state security in the region, and more equal bilateral cooperation as the pathway for its assumption of a 'normal' security role. The alliance partners have identified North Korea as a new common threat that variously serves both as a genuine rationale and a pretext for strengthening the alliance over the short term, and China's rise as a common threat that necessitates the upgrading of the alliance over the longer term.

Revision of the Japan–US Guidelines for Defence Cooperation

The first initiatives for strengthening the US–Japan alliance came from the US side, with the production of the 1995 East Asian Strategic Review, known as the 'Nye Report' after its principal sponsor, Joseph S. Nye, then US Assistant Secretary of State. The report focused upon the revitalisation of the US–Japan alliance as the keystone for US security strategy in East Asia. The Nye Report and US efforts to strengthen the alliance were conducted in conjunction with Japan's own attempts to review its security posture after the Cold War. Japan's process of revising the NDPO was conducted with the Nye Report in hand, thereby explaining the frequent references to the US–Japan security arrangements in this new defence doctrine.[1] Following on from the Nye Report and the revised NDPO of 1995,

Japan and the US turned their attention to the revision of the 1978 Guidelines as the next step in reorienting the alliance to respond to post-Cold War regional contingencies. After his February 1996 summit with President Bill Clinton, then Prime Minister Ryutaro Hashimoto ordered an internal LDP investigation and MOFA and JDA consultations regarding the necessity of revision. The investigation took place against the background of the March 1996 Taiwan Strait crisis, and served to confirm for LDP, MOFA and JDA policymakers that a revision of the Defence Guidelines and a strengthened bilateral alliance to deal with regional contingencies were essential for Japan's security.

Japan's decision to revise the Defence Guidelines was made public with the announcement, on 17 April 1996, during Clinton's visit to Japan, of the 'US–Japan Joint Declaration on Security: Alliance for the Twenty First Century'. The Joint Declaration affirmed the commitment of both sides to common democratic values; stressed the importance of the alliance not just for the security of Japan but also, for the first time, of the entire Asia-Pacific region; and agreed to a joint bilateral study into the revision of the Defence Guidelines to establish modes of cooperation for dealing with Article 6-type situations in areas surrounding Japan ('shuhen'). The Joint Declaration welcomed the US's maintenance of 100,000 troops in the region; pledged Japan's continued provision of Host Nation Support (HNS) to the US; and noted that Japan and the US would cooperate in the study of BMD. At the same time as the Joint Declaration was signed, the US and Japan also signed the ACSA, which enabled Japan to provide logistical support to the US in peacetime exercises, and during international relief activities and UN-led PKO.

From June 1996 onwards, the Japan–US Subcommittee for Defence Cooperation (SDC), under the auspices of the ministerial-level SCC, conducted investigations into the revision of the Defence Guidelines. Final recommendations for the revisions were produced in September 1997. The fields for bilateral cooperation to deal with regional contingencies in areas surrounding Japan include activities to deal with refugee flows, non-combat evacuations, the enforcement of economic sanctions, the use of JSDF and civilian base facilities, minesweeping and rear area logistical support – all requested by the US during the first North Korean nuclear crisis, but which Japan was unable to provide. In April 1998, the Japanese government submitted a Defence Guidelines bill ('shuhen jitaiho'), along with revisions to the JSDF Law, to enable a legal framework to mobilise the JSDF and provide other support for the US in the event of a regional contingency that 'impacts upon' the security of Japan. After lengthy debate, and revisions connected with the need for Diet ex-post facto approval of JSDF dispatch in the event of a contingency, the bill was passed by both houses in May 1999. Since then, Japan and the US have been working on a new 'comprehensive mechanism' for coordinating bilateral military cooperation to handle regional contingencies.

The revised Defence Guidelines represent a significant upgrading of the alliance's capabilities to respond to Article 6-type regional contingencies by filling in the gaps in military operability exposed at the time of the nuclear crisis. In 1996, the Joint Declaration had indicated the possible 'regionalisation' of the alliance's functions by expanding its scope to encompass the entire Asia–Pacific region. The potential for the geographical expansion of the scope of the alliance was further hinted at by the deliberately vague definitions of the range of action in the revised Defence Guidelines. Japanese and US policymakers stress that the revised Defence Guidelines have not been designed to counter the threat from any specific state, and that the term 'shuhen' used in the Guidelines, revised NDPO and Joint Declaration is 'situational' rather than geographical. The Japanese government has argued that, even though the new Guidelines do contain a geographical element – in that the scope of their operation is likely to be close to Japan and is not envisaged as stretching as far as the Indian Ocean or Middle East – they do not involve a revision of Prime Minister Kishi's 1960 definition of the Far East and the range of the original security treaty. As noted in Chapter 1, this definition was designed to delimit the scope of the security treaty; it was geographically specific, designating the area north of the Philippines and including South Korea and Japan. However, Japanese governments since 1997 have preferred to stress Kishi's additional statements at the time: that definitions of 'shuhen' do not necessarily restrict the security treaty's range of action, because it is not possible to mark a definitive geographical line around Japan's security interests.

Japan's subtle shift in emphasis from geographical to situational definitions of its 'shuhen' carries important advantages for Japan and its US alliance partner. Firstly, it allows Japan, using the concept of situational need, to extend the range of action of the bilateral alliance beyond the traditional limits of the Far East, as defined in 1960 by Prime Minister Kishi, so as to incorporate, if necessary, the entire Asia–Pacific region as envisaged in the Joint Declaration (see map p. 13). Secondly, the concept of situational need introduces a crucial element of strategic ambiguity into the scope of the US–Japan security treaty, with the particular advantage of leaving the position of Taiwan and China undetermined in the revised Defence Guidelines. Under the 1960 definition of the Far East, Taiwan comes within the scope of the Defence Guidelines, and the events of 1996 demonstrated that a conflict in the Taiwan Strait is still of major concern to Japan and the US. However, the policy of both partners is to hedge against a possible military contingency involving China by strengthening the bilateral alliance, but at the same time, to avoid the overt designation of China as a threat to avoid antagonising it and endangering general policies of engagement. The concept of situational need enables Japan and the US to de-emphasise Taiwan's clear-cut geographical position as part of Japan's 'shuhen' and as within the range of the revised Guidelines, while retaining for the alliance the option of operating in the Taiwan Strait if there is deemed to be sufficient situational need.

The revision of the Defence Guidelines has been a vital step in the reconfirmation ('saikakunin') or redefinition ('saiteigi') of the US–Japan alliance, and demonstrates a relative decline in Japanese concerns about fulfilling a more balanced role in the alliance or entrapment in US regional strategy. Nevertheless, Japan's commitment to the redefined alliance has not been total: its role is still confined to non-combat, rear area functions; it has not yet openly breached the principle of the non-exercise of collective self-defence; and it continues to engage in elaborate double-hedging strategies vis-à-vis the US as well as potential adversaries. The concept of situational need, and the fact that Taiwan's status as an object of concern in the revised Defence Guidelines is left vague, serve not only to avoid antagonising China, but also provide Japan with an opt-out clause to avoid committing itself to supporting the US in a war against China over Taiwan, if it judges that there is not sufficient situational need. Clearly Japan is unlikely to exercise this option in anything other than extreme circumstances of entrapment, as it would spell the political and military death of the alliance.

Table 7 **Cooperation in areas surrounding Japan under the revised Defence Guidelines**		
Functions and fields		**Examples of items of cooperation**
Cooperation in activities initiated by either government	Relief activities and measures to deal with refugees	Transportation of personnel and supplies to the affected area
		Medical services, communications and transportation in the affected area
		Relief and transfer operations for refugees, and provision of emergency materials to refugees
	Search and rescue	Search-and-rescue operations in Japanese territory and at sea around Japan and information sharing related to such operations
	Non-combatant evacuation operations	Information sharing, and communication with and assembly and transportation of non combatants
		Use of JSDF facilities and civilian airports by US aircraft and vessels for the transportation of non-combatants
		Customs, immigration and quarantine of non-combatants upon entry into Japan
		Assistance to non-combatants in such matters as temporary accommodation, transportation and medical services in Japan
	Activities for ensuring the effectiveness of economic sanctions for the maintenance of international peace and stability	Inspection of ships based on UN Security Council resolutions for ensuring the effectiveness of economic sanctions and activities related to such inspections
		Information sharing

Table 7 **Cooperation in areas surrounding Japan under the revised Defence Guidelines** (continued)		
Functions and fields		**Examples of items of cooperation**
Japanese support for US forces' activities	Use of facilities	Use of JSDF facilities and civilian airports and ports for supplies and other purposes by US aircraft and vessels
		Reservation of spaces for loading/unloading of personnel and materials by the US and of storage areas at JSDF facilities and civilian airports and ports
		Extension of operating hours for JSDF facilities and civilian airports and ports for use by US aircraft and vessels
		Use of JSDF airfields by US aircraft
		Provision of training and exercise areas
		Construction of offices, accommodations, etc., inside US facilities and areas
	Supply*	Provision of materials (except weapons and ammunition) and POL (petroleum, oil and lubricants) to US aircraft and vessels at JSDF facilities and civilian airports and ports
		Provision of materials (except weapons and ammunition) and POL to US facilities and areas
	Transportation*	Land, sea and air transportation inside Japan of personnel, materials and POL
		Sea transportation to US vessels on the high seas of personnel, materials and POL
		Use of vehicles and cranes for transportation of personnel, vehicles and POL

* Rear area support

Table 7 **Cooperation in areas surrounding Japan under the revised Defence Guidelines** (continued)		
Functions and fields		**Examples of items of cooperation**
Japanese support for US forces' activities	Maintenance*	Repair and maintenance of US aircraft, vessels and vehicles
		Provision of repair parts
		Temporary provision of tools and materials for maintenance
	Medical services*	Medical treatment of casualties inside Japan
		Transportation of casualties inside Japan
		Provision of medical supply
	Security*	Security of US facilities and areas
		Sea surveillance around US facilities and areas
		Security of transportation routes inside Japan
		Information and intelligence sharing
	Communications*	Provision of frequencies (including satellite communications) and equipment for communications among relevant US and Japanese agencies
	Others*	Support for port entry/exit by US vessels
		Loading/unloading of materials at JSDF facilities and civilian airports and ports
		Sewage disposal, water supply, and electricity inside US facilities and areas
* Rear area support		Temporary increase of workers at US facilities and areas
US–Japan operational cooperation	Surveillance Minesweeping	Intelligence sharing Minesweeping operations in Japanese territory and on the high seas around Japan, and information and intelligence sharing on mines
	Sea and airspace management	Maritime traffic coordination in and around Japan in response to increased sea traffic
		Air-traffic control and airspace management in and around Japan

Sources: Boeichohen, *Boeihakusho 2003* (Tokyo: Zaimusho Insatsukyoku, 2003), p. 115

Nevertheless, throughout the debate on the revised Defence Guidelines, Japanese policymakers emphasised that Japan should retain the option to say 'no' to the US concerning the operation of the security treaty, and the possession of this latent, if drastic, veto is seen to restrain the US from taking Japanese support for granted and thus from taking hasty actions over Taiwan.

Okinawa, US bases and force realignments

The second major issue to rock the US–Japan alliance in the early 1990s, was the issue of US bases on Okinawa. Japanese and US policymakers attempted to defuse domestic political unrest over Okinawa by establishing, in November 1995, the Special Action Committee on Facilities and Areas in Okinawa (SACO) to examine ways to reduce the size and number of US bases in the prefecture. SACO issued a mid-term report on 15 April 1996, timed to coincide with President Clinton's visit to Japan. This recommended the relocation of the Futenma Marine Air Station at Ginowan, and a general reduction of 20% in the land area of US bases in Okinawa. SACO's final report in December 1996 recommended that the Futenma facilities should be moved to a floating heliport off the coast of Okinawa.

Japan's government has been desperate to suppress the Okinawa base problem. It is willing to outlay massive expense on the floating heliport concept and to provide economic stimulus packages to the prefecture as a means to indirectly secure cooperation over the base issue. Central government initiatives, such as plans for base relocations and economic assistance, have placated local anti-base sentiment to some degree, but eight years on from the SACO report, the issue remains unresolved. The floating heliport plan was scuttled by opposition from prefectural and municipal governments in Okinawa. In 1999, the mayor of Nago City accepted a new prefectural proposal for the construction of a permanent runway for military and civilian use on reclaimed coastal land, and agreement was reached on this plan between the prefecture and Japanese central government in August 2002. Futenma has thus yet to be relocated: the prefecture insists on a 15-year time limit on its operation, a condition to which the US is reluctant to agree; and in any case the construction of the airstrip is likely to take up to 10 years. The Okinawa base problem, although in abeyance, still has the potential to sap domestic support for the alliance. One sign of progress was the US's consultation with Japan in June 2004 over the possibility of relocating the artillery unit of the US Marine Corps to Hokkaido as part of its global realignment of troops, although this is likely to encounter heavy opposition from Hokkaido residents concerned about live-firing exercises. The US also proposed, in July 2004, that Futenma's functions might be relocated to the US Air Force base at Kadena on Okinawa. However, the Futenma controversy has since been reopened following the crash of a US Marine Corps helicopter at the Okinawa International University campus just outside the air station in August. The impact of crash was exacerbated by the fact that the US military denied Japanese police access to the site under the bilateral Status of Forces Agreement (SOFA) – reinforcing Japanese perceptions of the US's lack of sensitivity to local feelings and renewing calls for the speedy transfer of the base.

Since the late 1970s, the Japanese government has assumed increasing responsibility for the costs of US bases on its soil. These payments were officially termed HNS ('zaiNichi Beigun churyu keihi futan'); Shin Kanemaru, the then Director General of the JDA, dubbed them 'omoiyari yosan', or 'sympathy payments', to compensate for costs associated with the rise in value of the yen and general defence burden on the US. Since 1987, Japan and the US have signed a series of Special Agreements for HNS; since the mid-1990s, Japan has come to assume around two-thirds of the total costs of the stationing of US troops. Japan does not pay the salaries of US personnel, but pays for nearly 100% of the costs for civilian base workers, the construction of amenities for US personnel, and fuel, heat and lighting at US facilities.[2] Japan's tight defence budget threatened to complicate new negotiations over HNS following the expiry of the Special Agreement for 1996–2001. However, Japanese policymakers' belief in the importance of the alliance ensured that a new Special Agreement was signed for 2001–06 that extended the same conditions to the US. In April 2004, Japan and the US also concluded a revised SOFA, which is intended to facilitate the transfer of US servicemen suspected of crimes to the Japanese authorities, thus easing political tensions between the US military and local civilian populations around bases.

Whatever the outcome of ongoing Japan–US consultations on the realignment and funding of bases, it seems certain that facilities in Japan will become ever more central to US regional and global strategy. The US utilised its bases in Japan to deploy forces in the Gulf

War; the carrier *Kitty Hawk* home-ported in Japan participated in the current conflicts in Afghanistan and Iraq; fighter aircraft from Misawa in Aomori Prefecture and Kadena Air Base in Okinawa participated in the Iraq war; US Marines in Okinawa were sent as reinforcements to Iraq in January 2004; and Okinawa, in particular, remains crucial as a staging post for the US to project power across the Pacific to the Indian Ocean and Middle East. Consequently, it is not surprising that the US 2004 Global Posture Review (GPR) looks set to maintain or even boost the US presence in Japan, whereas other allies, including South Korea, face sizeable reductions of US forces. In recent talks, the US appears to have reassured Japan that it intends to preserve current troop levels in Japan of around 58,000 servicemen (including around 14,000 of the US 7th Fleet). The US is also looking to strengthen the importance of its bases in Japan, proposing that the command functions of the US Army I Corps, a rapid-deployment force covering the Asia–Pacific, be relocated from Washington State to Army Camp Zawa in Kanagawa Prefecture. In addition, the US has proposed that the command operations of the 13th Air Force headquartered in Guam, a key base for long-range bombers and tanker aircraft often deployed in the Middle East, should be integrated with those of the 5th Air Force Command at Yokota Air Base in Tokyo.[3] The ramifications of this would be that Japan would essentially serve as a frontline US command post for the Asia–Pacific and beyond. The increased concentration of command functions in Japan would also increase cooperation between US forces and the JSDF. Japan might resist these proposals, given that the scope of the command functions extends far beyond the Asia–Pacific and the stated scope of the US–Japan security treaty. However, increased US–Japan out-of-area cooperation since 11 September, and the fact that Japan has given the US a free hand to use bases for actions in the Middle East in the past, suggests that Japan might have to accept its enhanced role as a fulcrum for US military commands in the Asia–Pacific and beyond. Indeed, the US's desire to convert its bilateral regional alliance into one that functions to support its global security objectives could even lead to a redefining of the entire US–Japan security treaty. Japan and the US are now locked in negotiations, expected to last until Spring 2005, over how to reconcile the treaty's provisions with the GPR. One outcome could be the redefinition of the geographical scope of the treaty, although Japan's government will attempt, if possible, to resist this.

Ballistic Missile Defence

Japan has strengthened the basis of alliance cooperation through the revised Defence Guidelines, while leaving open the hedging option against entrapment. Japan–US alliance bonds, however, are to be tightened even further by BMD. This project has ramifications far wider than the revised Defence Guidelines: Japan will lose its hedging option, be forced to breach the ban on collective self-defence and be unable to extricate itself from alliance cooperation in the future.

Japan's flirtation with missile defence stretches back to the agreement of the Yasuhiro Nakasone administration in 1986 to participate in the 'Star Wars' Strategic Defence Initiative (SDI). This agreement became the basis for Strategic Defence Initiative Office (SDIO), and between 1989 and 1993, US and Japanese private defence contractors conducted a joint study on Western Pacific Missile Architecture (WESTPAC). Japanese government interest in BMD was driven by the proliferation of ballistic missile technologies globally and in East Asia. Partly in reaction to the experience of the Gulf War, when the US used the *Patriot* system (with, in fact, minimal success) to intercept Iraqi missiles, and partly in reaction to North Korea's test launches of *No-dong*-1 missiles in May 1990 and May 1993, Japan upgraded its existing *Patriot* surface-to-air missile (SAM) system to the PAC-2 anti-ballistic missile system, and currently has 24 PAC-2 batteries.

In September 1993, Japan and the US established a Theatre Missile Defence Working Group (TMDWG) under the auspices of the SCC. In June 1994, the US put forward proposals for bilateral collaboration in TMD development, leading to the establishment, again under the SCC, of a Bilateral Study on Ballistic Missile Defence (BSBMD) to investigate the technological feasibility of BMD systems. In total, between 1995 and 1998, the Japanese government devoted ¥560 million to BMD research. In addition, it commissioned private Japanese defence contractors to investigate key technologies. Nevertheless, until the 'Taepo-dong shock' of August 1998, the Japanese government remained reticent about fully committing itself to developing the BMD in cooperation with the US. In December 1998, the government approved joint research with the US, signing an exchange of notes on research in August 1999. This kicked off a joint research programme into four key BMD interceptor missile technologies: infrared seekers in missile nose cones; the protection of infrared seekers from heat generated in-flight; the Kinetic Kill Vehicle for the destruction of ballistic missiles; and the second stage rocket motor of the interceptor missile.

From 1999 onwards, Japanese policymakers were at pains to stress that Japan–US cooperation on BMD remained purely at the research stage, and that further government deliberations would be necessary before moving to actual development and deployment of a system. Japan originally envisaged that the BMD joint research phase would be completed in 2003–04, but delays in the US testing programmes and the reconfiguration of missile defence programmes by the new Bush administration pushed this back to 2006. JDA Director General Ishiba proved an enthusiastic proponent, stating in December 2002, after a meeting with US Secretary of Defence Donald Rumsfeld, that Japan was studying BMD with an 'eye toward a future move to development and deployment'.[4] Ishiba was subsequently rebuked by both Fukuda and Koizumi for these comments.[5]

As it has transpired, Japan's government has adopted a faster schedule than first envisaged for the deployment of a BMD system. Against the background of the renewed North Korean nuclear crisis, Koizumi stated in May 2003 that Japan might 'accelerate consideration' of its participation in a joint BMD programme with the US. In December 2003, Japan announced that it would procure an off-the-shelf BMD system from the US, while continuing to investigate the joint development with the US of future BMD technology.

As a result of this decision, Japan is set to acquire upper- and lower-tier BMD systems. The upper-tier system is the sea-based Navy Theatre Wide Defence (NTWD), now termed under the Bush administration the Sea-Based Midcourse System (SMD). NTWD carries the advantage of being sea mobile and having a large defended territorial footprint of up to 2,000 kilometres in diameter against a 1,000 kilometre medium-range ballistic missile such as North Korea's *No-dong*-1. NTWD employs as its platform AWS-equipped ships; its interceptor missile is an upgraded SM-3. For sensors, the NTWD system employs an upgraded SPY-1B/D phased array radar to detect and track missile trajectories and provide on-board cueing for interceptor missile launches. The AWS and SPY-1B/D can be supplemented by Airborne Warning and

Control Systems (AWACS) and E-2C surveillance aircraft equipped with infrared search and tracking (IRST). However, space-based infrared sensors and the early warning tactical information that they provide, in the detection of heat plumes from missiles in their boost phases and in calculating their exact launch point, are essential to a truly effective BMD system. The upgraded SPY-1B/D functions mainly to detect missile launches from post-boost and mid-course phases onwards that pass through their effective field of range. Hence, infrared space-based sensors and their ability to detect at the earliest possible time the launch point of missiles are invaluable in minimising the area for the SPY-1B/D radar to search and maximising the time available for it to do so. US Defence Support Programme (DSP) satellites, and the planned US Space Based Infrared System (SBIRS) High and Low are uniquely capable of providing this infrared early warning and off-board cueing. Given that a 1,000 kilometre-range ballistic missile has a boost phase lasting 70–110 seconds, and a total flight time of less than ten minutes, access to this infrared sensor information should greatly enhance the probability to successfully cue up the interceptor missiles.

Japan's upper-tier NTWD is to be reinforced by the lower tier PAC-3, intended to intercept missiles in their terminal phase, now termed by the US as the Terminal Defence Segment (TDS). PAC-3 has a smaller defended footprint, but its layering with the NTWD system offers an enhanced probability of preventing leakage in a missile shield. In addition, JDA Director General Ishiba even indicated, in May 2004, that Japan might cooperate with US research into laser technologies for boost phase intercept (BPI) BMD systems. BPI has the advantage that it may be able to destroy missiles when they are slowest moving in their launch phase and large enough to easily detect, as their various rocket stages have not yet separated, and that the warhead material from any destroyed missile should fall back over the territory from which it was launched.[6] Japan plans to procure the upgraded AWS, SPY-1B/D and SM-3 missiles from the US for deployment on one of its AWS-equipped destroyers by the start of 2007; it will deploy the BMD system on all six of these ships by 2011, and upgrade to the PAC-3 and acquire the necessary interceptor missiles by the end of 2007. In the meantime, Japan and the US will continue their joint programme into interceptor missile technologies. Japan's decision to take the plunge with BMD was motivated by a range of factors. Japan increasingly perceives North Korea's force of up to 100 *No-dong* missiles as a clear and present danger. Japan's total vulnerability to ballistic missile attack and North Korea's potential willingness to use these weapons against Japan was dramatically emphasised by the 1998 *Taepo-dong*-1 launch. Japanese policymakers are also clearly concerned over the long term by China's ballistic-missile capabilities, and even by Russia's residual missile force in the region. Japan's lack of retaliatory capacity, and its argument that BMD systems are purely defensive, means that BMD is seen as a means to counter the missile threat and to fit its exclusively defence-oriented policy. Japan also possesses many of the platforms for BMD: four AWS destroyers, with two more planned for the current MTDP, and PAC-2 missile batteries for upgrading.

Koizumi's government finally tipped in favour of the early procurement of BMD for two reasons. Firstly, US testing of SMD systems progressed relatively smoothly, and PAC-3 systems were argued to have worked effectively during the Iraq war. Secondly, Japan seems to have been sold on BMD by US arguments that the systems could be procured more cheaply than previously thought. Joint development of the SMD/NTWD system was originally estimated at nearly ¥1 trillion (US$8.35bn), but the cost of fitting out four AWS destroyers for NTWD is now estimated at ¥100bn (US$830.5m); although the total cost of the BMD programme, including NTWD, PAC-3 and upgrades to the BADGE BMC4I, was still calculated by the JDA in its 2003 budget request as ¥1.3 trillion.[7]

Japan's introduction of a BMD system has radical implications for its strategic posture in East Asia and vis-à-vis the US. The first is the exacerbation of Japan's adversary security dilemma with China. Chinese policymakers are concerned that Japan's development of a BMD system developed in conjunction with the US could negate China's nuclear deterrent by providing Japan with both a 'spear' and a 'shield'. The 'spear' of the US extended nuclear deterrent would be complemented by a BMD 'shield', allowing Japan deterrence by both punishment and denial vis-à-vis China. Chinese fears might in part be justified, as the NTWD system may have some residual or 'break out' capabilities to defend against Chinese ICBMs. Certainly, the US regards the NTWD/SMD component of its missile defence as part of a defensive shield against ICBMs.[8] In all likelihood, though, China could overcome the negation of its strategic nuclear arsenal through the employment of countermeasures and development of multiple independently targetable re-entry vehicles (MIRV) to overwhelm any BMD system.

China's concerns extend to the Japan's possible countering of its tactical ballistic missiles and involvement in the Taiwan issue. China's worst-case scenario would be the deployment by Japan, either individually or in conjunction with the US, of its sea-mobile NTWD system to defend Taiwan. In particular, China would fear the formation of a quasi-alliance amongst the US, Japan and Taiwan. If the US were to sell AWS and BMD technology to Taiwan, this could result in all three powers being equipped with fully interoperable equipment, so smoothing the way for three-way military cooperation. Japan's reluctance to become embroiled directly in a Taiwan Strait crisis makes this an unlikely scenario, except in the case of full-scale war. It is far more likely that Japan would use its BMD system to defend US forces operating in a Taiwan Strait crisis from bases in Japan – an action that would complicate any attempts by China to intimidate US forces in the region, short of initiating a war against Japan as well. China can ultimately overcome any BMD system through increasing its missile production, a relatively cheap process which would likely enable China to saturate and overcome any defence. Therefore, Japan's interest in BMD carries the risk of accelerating China's upgrading of its nuclear and conventional ballistic-missile capabilities and generating further momentum for a regional arms race.

Japan faces another set of strategic implications arising from BMD in terms of alliance security dilemmas vis-à-vis the US and the risks of entrapment in regional conflicts. Japan's enhanced risks of entrapment are essentially derived from its technological dependence on the US in BMD. Japanese optical and SAR satellites do not have the infrared capabilities to detect and track hostile missiles. Japan possesses AWACs but these do not have IRST; and the upgraded SPY-1B/D radar on AWS-equipped ships lacks sufficient capabilities for fully effective on-board cueing and operating any kind of stand-alone system. Japan has to rely on sensor information from US DSP and SBIRS satellites; to access this sensor information, it will need to ensure that its upgraded BMC4I is capable of inter-connection and data-linking with US system. In turn, this technological dependence, and the unprecedented need for Japan to inter-link and integrate its command-and-control systems with that of the US is likely to generate a BMD architecture that will serve to further subordinate Japan within US regional and global strategy. Japan's decision to opt for an off-the-shelf BMD system from the US, most probably black-boxed, is sure to compound these risks of technological and strategic subordination. In deploying a US-designed NTWD system that is highly dependent on information flows originating from US, Japan is acquiring a weapon system dependent on active US cooperation to function properly. Japan's entire strategic orientation, therefore, must be geared even further to the general appeasement of its US ally if it wishes to defend itself.

In addition, Japan's procurement of BMD is likely to create scenarios that will dictate closer tactical bilateral cooperation. Japan's possession of NTWD will give it, for the first time, a sea-mobile weapons system with a range of defensive power of close to 2,000 kilometres. It is likely to face increasing calls from the US to deploy this capability in support of the alliance in regional contingencies, and in expeditionary warfare in other theatres such as the Middle East.[9] Moreover, the technological nature of BMD means that Japan's policymakers will no longer be able to employ the type of ambiguity found in the revised Defence Guidelines to obfuscate the true extent of their military support for the US. The short time-frame – typically less than ten minutes – needed for a BMD system to respond to a missile launch means that there will be no time for Japan's political leaders to debate decisions on interceptor launches. Instead, Japan's government will have to provide JSDF commanders in the field with clear rules of engagement to deal with a range of pre-planned scenarios that would commit Japan to a conflict. All of this necessitates increased Japanese planning for regional contingencies, much of which will involve closer coordination with the US and revealing to it in more definite terms the types of scenarios that would trigger Japanese military support. These rules of engagement will also involve some softening of the principle of civilian control over the military, and provide commanders in the field with a more free-ranging role to support the US.

Finally, BMD systems have vital implications for Japan's prohibition on the exercise of the right of collective self-defence. Japanese policymakers are increasingly aware that BMD systems, in order to function effectively, demand the free flow of sensor information not only from the US side, but also reverse flows from the Japanese. For instance, in April 2004, the US requested that Japan make available sensor information from its upgraded FPS-4 radar stations to US Navy missile defence assets.[10] In June, the US suggested that the ASDF's Air Defence Command be moved to the US Air Force base at Yokota, its seeming intention to promote the integration of BMC4I systems for BMD.[11] In addition, from 2005 onwards, Japan and the US are to begin joint training for the exchange of information on missile tracking between their respective AWS-equipped ships.[12] Japan and the US carried out a similar exercise in the Rim of the Pacific (RIMPAC) exercises in July 2004. Japan's current interpretation of the ban on collective self-defence prevents this interchange of information, and it is unlikely to be able to negotiate a missile defence architecture with the US that obviates this issue. Japan will also find it increasingly hard to hold the line on collective self-defence, given the changed nature of US missile defence programmes. The Bush administration's incorporation of all missile systems into one multi-layered global system raises questions as to whether Japan's NTWD, with its possible 'break out' capabilities against ICBMs launched from East Asia against the US, could thus be viewed as functioning for purposes of collective self-defence. If Japan were to engage in BPI missile defences, then this would further strengthen the collective self-defence argument, as it would be impossible to determine if missiles shot down over their launch sites were targeted at Japan or another state.

Japan's December 2003 announcement on the procurement of a BMD system stated that it would be operated on the basis of Japan's 'independent judgement' and not for the defence of other states.[13] Japan has long hoped for the acquisition of an independent BMD system. Indeed, in August 2001, then JDA Director General, Gen Nakatani, expressed the hope that Japan would develop an 'independently' ('shutaiteki') operated system.[14] However, the increasing recognition of Japan's policymakers is that a joint BMD programme with the US is eventually likely to force greater strategic and tactical integration with the US and an end to the ban on collective self-defence. In turn, BMD's breaching of the ban on collective self-defence should open the way for more radical changes in the scope of US–Japan alliance cooperation in other contexts.

Conclusion

Japan is becoming a more 'normal' US ally in the post-Cold War period. It has finally established, through the revised Defence Guidelines, with still some degree of hedging, its support for the US in regional contingencies, and thereby forged a revised strategic bargain for the regionalisation of alliance functions. Through BMD, Japan will almost inextricably tighten its integration with US regional and possibly global military strategy. All this might seem unsurprising in the contexts of other alliance relationships, but for Japan, it is close to revolutionary. Japan is gradually losing its fear of entrapment along with its ability to practice elaborate hedging strategies; it is more accepting of the integration of its forces and command-and-control structure with those of the US, a move it has taken pains to avoid during the entire post-war period; and it is willing to specify its support for its ally in certain types of war-fighting situations.

The likely trajectory of the US–Japan security relationship is oriented towards tighter alliance cooperation. A foretaste of this trajectory, and hopes from the US side for enhanced cooperation, was provided by the October 2000 report of a bipartisan study group organised by the National Institute of Strategic Studies at the US National Defence University, entitled *The United States and Japan: Advancing Toward a More Mature Partnership*. The group was led by Joseph Nye (sponsor of the 1995 East Asian Strategic Review) and Richard Armitage, later appointed as Assistant Secretary of State under the Bush administration, and an acknowledged 'Japan handler'. The Nye–Armitage report proposed that the US–Japan alliance should develop into a relationship comparable with that of the US and UK. It urged improved cooperation in military technology, BMD and intelligence sharing, as well as an end to the Japanese ban on collective self-defence.[15]

Japan is now moving towards these positions. Debates on constitutional revision and BMD are leading to the end of the ban on collective self-defence. In addition, as will be made clear in the next chapter, Japan is now moving to strengthen alliance cooperation through US-led coalitions in Afghanistan and Iraq, a development seen by some to presage Japan's mirroring the alliance role of the UK.

Chapter 5

Japan, regional cooperation, multi-lateral security and the 'war on terror'

Japan took no direct or multilateral role in East Asian security during the Cold War. Rather, its contribution to regional security was channelled via the indirect and bilateral mechanism of the US–Japan security treaty, and its contribution to global security via exclusively diplomatic and financial support for UN activities. In the immediate post-Cold War period, Japan remained averse to participation in regional multilateral security frameworks, for fear that they would conflict with and undermine the bilateral alliance frameworks that had seemingly been so successful in maintaining stability in the past. For instance, Prime Minister Toshiki Kaifu, echoing US policymakers, stated in July 1990 that it was 'too early' for any type of multilateral security arrangement in the region.

From the early 1990s onwards, however, Japan's policymakers have undergone a conversion, and have been increasingly looking to participate in a range of frameworks for direct bilateral and multilateral security cooperation with other states in East Asia and beyond, and at the UN level. Japan's new interest in regional multilateralism can be attributed to the collapse of the USSR, which ended any fears that proposals for multilateralism emanating from this quarter could undermine the bilateral alliance with the US, and to Japan's concerns to find new ways to engage the US in the region. Multilateralism was also a means to expand Japan's security presence while reassuring other regional states about its intentions.[1] Japan now argues that the US–Japan bilateralism of the security treaty is complementary with multilateralism – the alliance providing an essential platform of stability and confidence upon which can be constructed mutually reinforcing layers of bilateral and multilateral security cooperation.[2]

Japan's 'multi-tiered' conception of regional security cooperation, together with the expanded scope of its participation in UN PKO and its recent involvement in US-led multilateral operations in Afghanistan and Iraq, mark important developments in its postwar security policy. Japan's experimentation with regional bilateral and multilateral frameworks, as well as being a valuable direct contribution to regional security, might offer Japan a long-term option to counter-balance or even break its dependence on the US in security matters. Similarly, Japan's participation in UN PKO and attachment to UN principles offers another potential means for Japan to move out of the US's security shadow, and even to constrain US dominance over multilateral institutions or tendencies towards unilateralism.

In fact, though, the evidence from the past decade suggests that Japan's policymakers have little real interest in fostering new bilateral and multilateral activities as constraints upon or alternatives to US–Japan alliance cooperation. Instead, as elucidated below, Japan's continued prioritisation of the bilateral alliance as the core of its security policy has meant that it has tended to treat regional multilateral frameworks as, at best, supplementary to the alliance and, more usually, as entirely subordinate. In certain instances, Japan's attachment to bilateral frameworks has actually subverted multilateral frameworks, with the prioritisation of the former undermining the ability of the latter to develop. With regard to other emergent regional multilateral frameworks, such as the ARF, and Japanese participation in UN PKO and the 'war on terror', Japan's exploration of multilateralism is designed more to ultimately strengthen bilateral cooperation with the US. In no way do Japanese policymakers seriously contemplate multilateralism as providing an alternative or even rival to the bilateralism of the security treaty.

Bilateral regional security dialogue

Since the late 1980s, Japan has conducted regular exchanges and consultations of high-level political, bureaucratic and uniformed defence officials up to the ministerial level with a number of ASEAN states, South Korea and China. Its 'defence diplomacy' has included mutual naval visits and joint search-and-rescue exercises with South

Korea.[3] Japan's confidence-building measures have contributed greatly to dispelling suspicion in Southeast Asia of its remilitarisation. Japan–South Korea security cooperation has been driven forward by common concerns over North Korea and by increased interaction of commercial shipping in overlapping EEZs that necessitates clearer maritime cooperation. Given the strong anti-Japanese sentiment in South Korea, a legacy of the country's time as a Japanese colony (1910–45), progress has been remarkable. Nevertheless, the state of Japan–South Korea security cooperation remains delicate: South Korea cancelled military exchanges to be held in June 2001 in protest at its perception of historical distortion in Japanese school texts that tread lightly on the delicate subject of Japan's colonial past. Similarly, Japan–China security cooperation has not always gone smoothly. Tensions over Tiananmen Square, China's 1995 nuclear tests and the revised Defence Guidelines made for a stop–start pattern in security dialogue. In January 2004, China refused a Japanese proposal for exchange visits between the MSDF and the People's Liberation Army Navy because of tensions over Koizumi's visit to the Yasukuni Shrine to pay his respects to Japanese war dead.[4]

Anti-piracy cooperation

The issue of piracy has provided an opportunity for Japan further to boost security cooperation with ASEAN states. Since the end of the Cold War, Japan, being reliant on the security of SLOCs for trade and resources, has become concerned about the rising incidence of piracy in East Asia. It is also concerned about the threat of maritime terrorism, such as a potential hijacking of Japanese shipments of mixed oxide (MOX) nuclear fuel from Europe. The Ministry of Land, Infrastructure and Transport reported that incidents of piracy involving Japan-related shipping increased from one in 1989 to 39 in 1999 and 31 in 2000, falling back to 10 in 2001.[5] Around 75% of these attacks took place in East Asian waters, and within this region close to 100% were in Southeast Asian waters. Japanese citizens have been injured in these attacks, and in a some cases, pirates have seized entire ships and set their crews adrift. The Japanese government attributes the rise in piracy to a combination of the reduced presence of US and Russian naval forces in the South China Sea since the end of the Cold War and the 1998 East Asian financial crisis, which has increased the incentives for criminal activity.

Japan has responded at the regional level with a variety of anti-piracy initiatives. At the November 1999 Japan-ASEAN summit, it proposed the initiation of a meeting of coast guard representatives to discuss the issue of piracy. In April 2000, Japan hosted the first Regional Conference on Combating Piracy and Armed Robbery Against Ships. This conference adopted the 'Tokyo Appeal', the 'Model Action Plan to Combat Piracy and Armed Robbery Against Ships' and the 'Asia Anti-Piracy Challenges 2000' documents. These emphasised the importance of regional cooperation against piracy; outlined specific measures for shipping security, including improved reporting and exchange of information on piracy between governments; and recommended bilateral and multilateral coast-guard cooperation. In September 2000, Japan dispatched survey teams to the Philippines, Malaysia, Singapore and Indonesia. A meeting of piracy experts was held in Malaysia in November of the same year; and from April 2001, Japan accepted foreign students at the JCG Academy. In November 2000, at the ASEAN Plus Three (APT), Japan subsequently proposed a second regional piracy conference, the Asian Cooperation Conference on Combating Piracy and Armed Robbery Against Ships, which was held in Tokyo in October 2001. In November 2001, Japan proposed at the APT summit the formation of a working experts group on anti-piracy measures.

These Japanese initiatives have generated some important bilateral progress in combating piracy. JCG ships visited Singapore, the Philippines and Thailand in the period August–December 2001 and conducted bilateral training exercises with each of these states' coastguards, as well as patrols in international waters. Since 2001, Japan has received requests from the Philippines to supply multi-purpose ships to the Philippine Coast Guard. In November 2002, the two states conducted joint coast-guard training exercises that involved JCG personnel storming a hijacked vessel. In July 2002, the JCG announced its dispatch of a 5,300-tonne patrol ship carrying two helicopters to conduct joint drills with the Brunei's Marine Police, and the dispatch of a *Falcon* 900 surveillance aircraft to Malaysia, Singapore and Indonesia for joint drills and patrols.[6]

How far Japan can extend the scope of its anti-piracy activities and promote multilateral cooperation on this issue is, however, questionable. China apparently suspects that Japan may be utilising JCG activities as a means to justify the expansion of its naval presence in the region and pave the way for the MSDF to compensate for any potential decline in US regional patrols. These suspicions may not be totally unjustified, given that Japan's interest in anti-piracy operations in part originated from the JDA establishment. The JDA's National Institute of Defence Studies (NIDS) conducted research in 1997 into the possibility of MSDF anti-piracy patrols with ASEAN states as part of 'ocean peacekeeping operations' (OPK).[7] This would have represented a major expansion of MSDF responsibilities beyond the 1,000 nautical-mile patrol range adopted in 1981 at the height of the renewed Cold War. Meanwhile, some ASEAN states are also believed to have encouraged Japan's efforts not only to counter piracy per se, but to engage Japan as a potential naval power in the region to counter China's influence in the South China Sea.[8] Japan's current policy is clearly limited to anti-piracy activities, and it has moved cautiously to ensure that China is not provoked. Nevertheless, then JDA Director General Ishiba referred to OPK and joint patrols with other East Asian states at the IISS-hosted Shangri-la Dialogue in 2003 and again in 2004. In sum, Japan is constructing frameworks for bilateral cooperation with the ASEAN states on piracy that, over the longer term, could be the basis for more substantial naval cooperation and a larger Japanese military presence in Southeast Asia.

Multilateral security dialogue and exercises

Japan's new belief in the importance of multilateral security dialogue was dramatically revealed by Foreign Minister Taro Nakayama's proposal at the July 1991 ASEAN-Post Ministerial Conference that, in the future, the meeting should become a 'forum for political dialogue … designed to improve the sense of mutual security' among East Asian states. At the time, Nakayama's initiative was greeted coolly by the ASEAN states. Nonetheless, in conjunction with earlier ASEAN-Institutes of Strategic and International Studies (ASEAN-ISIS) proposals, it did become the basis for the July 1993 agreement to create the ARF.

Japan has proved to be a staunch supporter of the ARF process since its inception. MOFA officials have taken regular part in ARF Senior Officials Meetings and Inter-Sessional Meetings on PKO, and in 1997 co-chaired, with Indonesia, the Inter-Sessional Support on confidence-building measures. Japanese academics and policymakers have taken part in the Track II Council for Security Cooperation in the Asia Pacific (CSCAP) to support the ARF. The Japan Institute of International Affairs (JIIA), a research institute affiliated with MOFA, has directed Japan's participation in CSCAP, co-chairing the North Pacific Working Group and providing the largest share of funding to overall CSCAP activities. JIIA researchers take part also in the Track II US–Japan–Russia Trilateral Forum on North Pacific Security; and Japanese MOFA and JDA officials take part in a Track II capacity in the Northeast Asia Cooperation Dialogue (NEACD), involving Japan, the US, South Korea and Russia.

In recent years, other multilateral security dialogue fora have proliferated in the East Asia region with the participation and sponsorship of Japan. Since 1996, the JDA has hosted the Forum for Defence Authorities in the Asia–Pacific Region, involving bureau-chief level officials from across East Asia. The JSDF has hosted a number of seminars for military officers since the mid-1990s, including the Pacific Armies Management Seminar (PAMS) and Western Pacific Naval Symposium (WPNS), held in Japan in 2000 and 2002 respectively. The National Defence Academy has hosted an international cadets' conference since 1998, and NIDS the Asia–Pacific Security Seminar since 1994.

In 1997, the Japanese government first put forward the concept of six-party dialogue on Korean Peninsula security issues, later realised by US initiatives in 2003, with Japan as a full participant. Since 2002, Japan has actively backed the IISS's Asia Security Conference, or Shangri-la Dialogue. This provides a new venue for defence minister-level discussions; in 2002, then JDA Director Gen Nakatani even suggested that it be converted into a formal Asia–Pacific Defence Ministerial Meeting to complement the largely foreign ministry-centred ARF. Japan has further backed multilateral security cooperation in a number of other frameworks with less traditional security or broader functions. From 1995, Japan has been a key partner, alongside the US, South Korea, the EU and a number of ASEAN and Asia–Pacific states, in KEDO, pledging up to US$1bn for the construction of light-water reactors to help eliminate North Korea's nuclear programme. In addition, Japan has utilised Asia-Pacific Economic Cooperation (APEC), an organisation not originally designed for security purposes, as a forum to discuss issues such as North Korea's missiles.

Japan's support for the ARF and the emergent alphabet soup of multilateral security frameworks in East Asia represents an important turn-around in its previous resistance to multilateralism. However, Japan's commitment to multilateralism within the overall scheme and trajectory of its security policy, and especially vis-à-vis its strengthening commitment to the US–Japan bilateral alliance, remains very limited. It is important to note that Japan is only able to contemplate participation in multilateral frameworks because they function not to supplant but to supplement the existing US–Japan bilateral arrangement at the core of its security policy. The ARF and other frameworks are acceptable to Japan because they stop at the level of cooperative security and dialogue, and do not demand any type of defence commitment that could clash with commitments under the US–Japan security treaty. As a result, their effectiveness as security guarantors, in their present incarnation, is very constrained (for example, the ARF's mandate even to discuss key regional security issues such as the Spratly islands and Taiwan is extremely narrow). Given the limitations of the ARF and other regional frameworks for security cooperation, and in face of the North Korean threat and the looming Chinese one, Japanese policymakers do not entertain any conception of multilateralism as a credible alternative to the bilateral US–Japan alliance. In their view, the US–Japan alliance is the only immediate and reliable guarantee of security available.

Japan's experimentation with multilateralism as a means to supplement and even boost bilateral cooperation with the US is demonstrated by a range of other recent multilateral activities. The US–Japan–South Korea Trilateral Coordination and Oversight Group (TCOG) process has provided Japan with a form of direct and multilateral framework for influencing Korean Peninsula security affairs. It could even be viewed as the culmination of the process of the creation of a 'quasi' or 'virtual' alliance among the three dialogue partners.[9] Similarly, Japan has taken part in the Trilateral Security Dialogue (TSD) with the US and Australia since August 2002. TCOG and the TSD represent another advance in multilateralism in East Asia, but these frameworks are essentially given life by the US. The US retains the prime leadership role, and these frameworks only serve to connect a selected number of spokes on selected issues of the bilateral alliance system in the region, leaving the US very much its dominant hub. Japan's participation in multilateral military exercises in the region tells a similar story. Japan has participated in RIMPAC exercises since 1980, and has sent observers to the *Cobra Gold* exercises in Southeast Asia since 2001. Japan has tended to treat its role as the conduct of a bilateral exercise with the US alongside a multilateral exercise, so as to lessen concerns about the exercise of collective self-defence. Clearly, Japan is gaining experience through these exercises of operations in a general multilateral environment. But once again, it is multilateralism centred on the US and its bilateral alliance networks, rather than multilateralism as an alternative and separate model for regional security cooperation.

Hence, the US, in hegemonic fashion, still mediates relations among its bilateral alliance partners, and uses trilateral multilateralism to buttress rather than move away from its existing 'hub and spokes' system. Japan and the US view multilateralism in East Asia as a supplemental 'bolt-on' accessory, which adds new functions but should not effect fundamentally the nature of bilateralism and its core role in regional security. In certain cases, this can be termed as a policy of 'bilateralism-plus', 'enriched bilateralism', or perhaps more appropriately 'depleted multi-lateralism'.[10]

Moreover, it is arguable that Japan's prioritisation of the bilateral US–Japan alliance over regional multilateralism has meant that, in certain circumstances, frameworks such as the ARF – at best, merely supplemental to the alliance – can be denied even these supplemental functions. The ARF is a cooperative security dialogue body that works on the principle that none of the participants identify each other as an adversary. However, efforts by Japan and the US to strengthen their alliance, and the well-understood fact that, despite Japanese hedging and obfuscation tactics, China is the object of this strengthened alliance, contravenes this principle. The reluctance of Japan and the US to commit themselves to multilateralism and their favouring of bilateralism are key contributory factors in China's similar reluctance to commit itself to the ARF as its preferred form of multilateral cooperation in the region. As a result, the potential function of the ARF is weakened all around. From this perspective, it becomes clear that the US–Japan bilateral alliance, rather than serving as a basis for the development of regional multilateralism, may actually serve as a ceiling to it.[11]

Japan and UN PKO

Japan's passing of the IPCL in June 1992 enabled the first dispatch of the JSDF on non-combat UN PKO missions to Cambodia in September 1992–September 1993. Japan's human contribution to the UN Transitional Authority Cambodia (UNTAC) took the form of deployments of 36 civilian election observers, 75 civilian police officers and 600 GSDF engineers for supply and reconstruction projects. Following on from UNTAC, Japan has participated in UN PKO and relief operations in Mozambique (1993–95), Rwanda (1994) and the Golan Heights (1996 to the present day). Japan's next participation in UN PKO in East Asia was in East Timor: it dispatched monitors to the 2001 elections, and in the period 2002–04, committed 680 GSDF personnel for reconstruction activities.

Japan has begun to expand the scope of its UN PKO activities. In 2002, it 'unfroze' provisions in the IPCL that had limited its participation in 'core' UN PKO, enabling it to take part in the monitoring of ceasefires, the patrol of ceasefire zones, the inspection, transport and disposal of weapons, and the exchange of prisoners. The Japanese government's Advisory Group on International Cooperation for Peace reported that Japan should improve coordination among relevant ministries involved in PKO and make more efficient use of ODA for a smoother progression from conflict prevention to peace consolidation.

Japan's new-found role in UN PKO is an important contribution to regional and international security and provides Japan with a 'normal' role on a par with other UN members. It is a realisation, in part, of the UN-centred security policy long espoused in the BPND. Japan has the capacity to undertake considerably more UN PKO in the future, given that its wholly professional military is comparable in size to that of the UK or France, and the fact that, to date, JSDF deployments have been relatively limited in the number of personnel and the scope of their activities. Japan's role in UN-centred international security activities, as explained in the following sections, could be further expanded through the concept of collective security to include non-traditional PKO, such as peace enforcement.

In fact, though, as explained in the following section from the evidence of the 'war on terror', Japan will continue to expand its role in PKO, but with less emphasis on UN-centred PKO per se and more operations styled as 'PKO within US-led coalitions' with varying degrees of UN legitimisation. Japan often appears to be borrowing the language and concomitant legitimacy of UN PKO, and precedents for dispatch of the JSDF established under UN mandates, as a means to push forward incrementally enhanced US–Japan alliance cooperation. Hence, JSDF participation in PKO, not as 'blue helmets', but as members of US-inspired coalitions, may open the way for greater multilateral interaction with other states. But essentially, this multilateralism is driven by US-centred interests, ultimately creating expanded opportunities for the enhanced bilateralism that remains at the core of Japan's security. Once again, then, multilateralism serves as a supplement rather than as an alternative to US-centred alliance cooperation.

Japan and the 'war on terror' in Afghanistan and Iraq
JSDF deployment to the Afghan campaign

Japan's reaction to 11 September and the impending US-led international campaign against al-Qaeda and transnational terrorism, as already noted in Chapter 2, was to swiftly enact the ATSML in October 2001. Working from the ATSML, the Japanese government then devised a Basic Plan enabling JSDF deployment from November 2001 to support the campaign in Afghanistan. The ATSML originally designated JSDF operations as lasting six months until May 2002, but the Basic Plan under the law has subsequently been revised six times to extend JSDF dispatch in six-month blocs up to May 2005. Under the Basic Plan, the JSDF's range of action was defined as including not just the sea and airspace of the Indian Ocean itself, but the land territory of the states located along the coast of the Indian Ocean and the supply lines stretching back to Japan, Australia and the US. MSDF flotillas (comprising fuel supply and transport ships and two destroyers), in combination with ASDF transport aircraft, have been charged with providing refuelling and logistical transport, and medical and maintenance support to US and other forces in the Indian Ocean and Arabian Sea. The MSDF's original mission was to supply fuel to the US and UK, but from November 2002 onwards the list of recipient navies was expanded to include Germany, New Zealand, France, Italy, the Netherlands, Spain, Canada and Greece. As of October 2004, the MSDF had provided, free of charge, on 430 occasions to coalition ships fuel totalling 375,000 kilolitres.[12] The MSDF has transported humanitarian supplies for Afghan refugees via Karachi in Pakistan, and in November 2002, carried Thai army transport construction machinery to the Indian Ocean for the repair of US airfield facilities in Afghanistan. The ASDF has flown supplies for the US military from US bases in Japan to staging posts such as Guam. Under the Basic Plan, the GSDF was provided with a potential but never-exercised role in the Afghan campaign – the provision of medical treatment to refugees and US personnel in neighbouring Pakistan.

To realise the ATSML and this set of JSDF missions in support of the US and international community, Japan was obliged to supersede previous security legislation and circumvent its own constitutional prohibitions. Japanese policymakers initially considered, but then rejected, the utilisation of the revised Defence Guidelines as a readily available framework to provide support for their US ally. Firstly, the revised Guidelines were regarded as overly restrictive of JSDF activities: the rationale for their activation was a military contingency that, if left unaddressed, would have a direct impact on Japan's security, a difficult case to argue in the instance of Afghanistan. Moreover, Japan's government had stated, since 1999, that the Indian Ocean was not envisaged as being within the scope of the revised Guidelines. Furthermore, Japanese policymakers' investigation of the possibility of dispatching the GSDF would have been effectively blocked by the revised Guidelines, which limited JSDF support for the US to sea and airspace. Secondly, the revised Guidelines were regarded as under-restrictive in that, if utilised for the Afghan campaign, a new precedent would be set for JSDF dispatch that would have undermined previous Japanese government efforts to retain control over the geographical and functional scope of its military and thereby to limit the risk of entrapment in regional contingencies.

Japan's search for a legal framework to enable JSDF dispatch was complicated by the hurdle of collective self-defence. The US and its NATO allies justified their involvement in the Afghan campaign primarily on the rights of individual and collective self-defence, rather than on existing UN resolutions. Japan might have been able to invoke the right of individual self-defence based on the number of Japanese fatalities in the 11 September attacks, but this would have likely mandated a combat role for the JSDF. Japan's exercise of the right of collective self-defence was not a constitutional option.

Instead, Japan's preference has been for a non-combat and logistical role that invokes neither the right of individual or collective self-defence but which is predicated on relevant UN resolutions. Japan has stressed UN resolutions that identify the 11 September attacks on the US as a threat to international peace, and which call on all UN members, and by implication Japan as well, to counter terrorism. Japan has been able to link this UN legitimacy to its own constitution to legitimise JSDF dispatch by switching emphasis from Article 9 of the Constitution to the Preamble. The Preamble states that Japan should work with international society for the preservation of peace. Japan has used the Preamble to argue that it should support the UN, as international society's highest representative, and its relevant resolutions to counter terrorism. In turn, Japan bridged UN resolutions, its constitution and support for the US by stressing that its support was not just for the US but for the whole international community to fight terrorism. The extraordinarily convoluted full name of the ATSML, which emphasises support for the US and international society, manifests this desire to wrap up its bilateral support for the US firmly within the legitimating context of the UN.[13]

JSDF dispatch to Iraq

Japan's response to the Iraq war took the initial form, in March 2003, of Prime Minister Koizumi's expression of 'understanding' for the military action; promises to extend JSDF commitments to the Indian Ocean under the ATSML to free up US forces for operations in Iraq; and provision of humanitarian assistance to Iraq and neighbouring states during the war. In the run-up to President Bush's declaration of the end of major combat operations in May 2003, Japanese policymakers had already turned their attention to Iraqi post-war reconstruction, dispatching fact-finding missions to consider the type of humanitarian and reconstruction assistance required. The Japanese government waited for the passing of UN Resolution 1483 in May calling upon members to assist in the reconstruction of Iraq and then, after only five weeks of deliberation, passed through the Diet, by July 2003, the LCSMHRA, which provided for JSDF dispatch on non-combat reconstruction missions.

Japan's final commitment to JSDF dispatch was held up by the House of Representatives elections in November 2003, during which Prime Minister Koizumi watched for any adverse public reaction to the prospect of an Iraq deployment. The general deterioration of the security situation in Iraq from mid-2003 onwards was also a restraining factor. Japan is believed to have rejected as too risky original US requests for GSDF deployment to Balad, north of Baghdad; and to have considered instead deployment to the relatively peaceful Kurdish-controlled north. In November 2003, Japan settled on Samawah in al-Muthana Province, southwest of Basra, as the most stable site for GSDF deployment. Bomb attacks in the same month upon Italian troops in Nasiriyah, approximately 100 kilometres east of Samawah, pushed back plans for dispatch to early 2004. However, the killing of two Japanese diplomats later in the month on the road to Tikrit hardened the resolve of policymakers to seek JSDF dispatch. In mid-December, a Basic Plan was formulated under the LCSMHRA for JSDF dispatch to Iraq, scheduled to run for one year. Japan also signed an exchange of letters for a SOFA-type agreement with Kuwait in December for the passage of Japanese troops through its territory (Qatar had rejected similar SOFA proposals at the same time). The final go-ahead for deployment was provided by the visit to Samawah of Takenori Kanzaki, the New Komeito leader and key LDP coalition partner, who vouched for the safety of the site.

In enacting the LCSMHRA and committing itself to JSDF, the Japanese government put forward a dual rationale. As Koizumi stated upon the announcement of the Basic Plan, deployment to Iraq was essential for maintaining confidence in the US–Japan bilateral alliance, a vital mechanism for Japan's own security. The rationale of alliance preservation was presented in parallel with the need to assist the international community's effort in the reconstruction of Iraq, although, as in the case of the Afghan campaign, the priority of Japanese policymakers often appears to be to utilise language referring to the 'international community', and by association the UN, to facilitate alliance cooperation, rather than to fulfil the actual needs of a broader international community beyond that centred on the US. In his announcement, Koizumi conflated the US and UK with the 'international community', giving the obfuscating impression of a broad-based coalition on a par with the previous Afghan campaign. The LCSMHRA itself was justified on the basis of UN Resolutions 1458 and 1511, lending legitimacy to Japan's participation in the US-led campaign, even though the degree of UN and international legitimacy conferred by these resolutions was actually relatively weak. Finally, Koizumi employed the same constitutional circumvention, as in the Afghan campaign, to link Japan's support (essentially directed towards its bilateral ally) with the domestically vaunted legitimacy of the UN and its own constitution. Koizumi stressed the constitutionality of JSDF deployment, but chose to read out in support of this argument not Article 9 as the previous arbiter of Japan's security, but instead, the Preamble.[14] Hence, JSDF deployment to Iraq, which derives its essential legitimisation from UN-centred multilateralism, appears once again as a mission to supplement the needs of the US–Japan alliance. As then JDA Director General Ishiba stated at the time of the dispatch of the main GSDF contingent to Iraq in January 2004, 'This is an operation to solidify confidence in Japan–US relations. The only organisation capable of doing this is the JSDF'.[15]

JSDF began deployment with the despatch of a 30-member GSDF advance team in mid-January 2003, concluding with the staged deployment overland via Kuwait of the main 600-member contingent between late February and late March. The GSDF constructed a fortified camp in Samawah, and from March onwards has been engaged in the provision of medical care, the purification and distribution of water, the repair of water supplies, and the reconstruction of public amenities such as schools and hospitals. The GSDF, in addition to its normal armament on overseas deployment of pistols, rifles and machine guns, has been permitted to arm itself with recoilless rifles and light anti-tank munitions, as well as wheeled APCs and light armoured vehicles to counter the threat of insurgent suicide attacks. However, despite this being the most heavily armed overseas deployment of Japanese ground troops in the post-war period, the GSDF's strict rules of engagement for self-defence mean that in most instances, it has relied on the protection of Dutch troops.[16] All the indications are that the JSDF has worked with great professionalism in the Samawah area, although struggling with unreal expectations from local Iraqi citizens about the employment opportunities that Japanese aid might bring, and with a deteriorating security environment.

Since February 2004, around 200 ASDF personnel have been engaged in transporting humanitarian and reconstruction supplies on C-130s from Kuwait to Iraq. The ASDF's original mission parameters under the Basic Plan includes airlifting to Baghdad, Balad, Mosul and Basra. In addition, although the JSDF cannot transport ammunition for US troops, ASDF commanders in April 2004 stated that they had transported armed US troops to Iraq.[17] Nonetheless, the Japanese government appears to have been reluctant to allow the ASDF to fly into the Baghdad area because of the high security risk, and the ASDF has concentrated on supplying the GSDF in Samawah via Nasiriyah or Basra. Since February this year, the MSDF has used its *Osumi* amphibious landing ship to ferry supplies from Japan to Kuwait for the GSDF.

Implications of the 'war on terror': crossing the Rubicon?

Japan's participation in the 'war on terror' contains potentially radical implications for its overall security policy trajectory, especially its multilateral security role and the US–Japan alliance. For some observers, Japan is now seen to have reached the point of no return in moving towards acting as a 'normal' military power, a partner for international security cooperation and a more committed US ally.[18] Japan's radicalism in the 'war on terror' and degree of departure from its previous incremental trajectory of expanding its security responsibilities should not be overstated. In devising their response to the Afghan campaign and Iraq war, Japanese policymakers have remained wary of entrapment in US-inspired military contingencies and have continued to pursue hedging options. Japan has predicated the ATSML and LCSMHRA as the legal frameworks for JSDF deployment upon relevant UN resolutions, even if the strength of these resolutions differs greatly between the Afghanistan and Iraq contexts. Moreover, the Japanese government has ensured that each JSDF dispatch to Afghanistan and Iraq is enabled by separate laws. The ATSML and LCSMHRA, although in part using the revised Defence Guidelines as a template for functional operations, are separate from the legal framework of the US–Japan security treaty. In using UN resolutions as the overt trigger for JSDF deployment, Japan has thus created an escape clause to avoid involvement in US-led operations that it views as not having a strong UN mandate, as in the case of the invasion of Iraq. Japan's use of separate laws for each JSDF deployment has erected a set of firewalls between each mission, enabling it to simultaneously push forward but also limit on a case-by-case basis the extent of support that it provides to the US under the ATSML, the LCSMHRA and the bilateral security treaty. Japan's desire to prevent any form of open-ended commitment to the Afghan and Iraq campaigns is shown also by the limited, although extendable, time frames placed on the expiry of both laws, and by the need for Diet ex-post facto approval of dispatch.

Japan's continued hyper-caution in committing its military forces to overseas actions is further demonstrated by the types of missions and capabilities chosen for the JSDF. The JSDF under the ATSML and LCSMHRA are deployed in non-combat zones ('sento koi ga okanwarete orazu') to limit the risks of embroilment in a conflict. The Japanese government found it easier to argue this distinction in the case of Afghanistan, with the MSDF as the main deployment and with no eventual need to risk GSDF deployment to Pakistan. In the case of Iraq, prior to JSDF deployment, and despite its best efforts to a find a safe zone in Samawah, the government found the argument that the GSDF would be dispatched to a non-combat zone hard to sell to the Japanese public. Since the GSDF's deployment to Iraq, it has trodden very cautiously, avoiding involvement in any form of combat. Media reports that a single anti-personnel landmine was found near the projected site for the GSDF Samawah camp in February 2004, but that this was not included in the GSDF assessments of the safety of the area, were sufficient to cause disquiet in Japan over the mission.[19] The GSDF, as noted above, has relied in the first instance on the Dutch for protection, and as the security situation around Samawah has deteriorated, including mortar attacks from April onwards near and on its camp, it has curtailed many of its activities and shut itself up in base.[20]

JSDF capabilities also remain limited, thereby curtailing the risks of being co-opted into combat duties. The GSDF in Iraq has a force structure and armaments that only serve for self-defence, and remains firmly under sole Japanese command. The specific numbers of troops deployed and the type and numbers of their equipment is strictly laid down under the ATSML and LCSMHRA to the last light-armoured vehicle and bulldozer. Most famously, and much to the chagrin of the US, Japan's government decided not to dispatch the MSDF's AWS destroyers to the Indian Ocean area in its first deployments in November 2001. It only relented in December 2002, sending two AWS destroyers in rotation. Japanese policymakers were deeply divided on the issue of Aegis dispatch. On the one hand, they recognised that the AWS destroyers are the MSDF's most capable asset, providing it with maximum flexibility and security in an uncertain theatre of operations. On the other hand, they were concerned that the high degree of inter-operability and data-linking systems between MSDF and US Navy warships equipped with the AWS might lead to US requests for Japan to deploy its naval assets as substitutes for those of the US. This would highlight problems of the exercise of collective self-defence and would pose the risk that Japanese forces might become directly involved in combat operations. The Japanese government eventually took the decision for deployment only after persistent internal pressure from MOFA, the JDA and the MSDF, all of whom sought to maximise the safety of Japanese forces and the degree of visible support for the US-led war effort. The deployment also came after the dampening down of hostilities in Afghanistan, minimising the risks that the MSDF would become involved in combat operations.

In the 'war on terror', Japan has not yet crossed its Rubicon, and continues to pursue cautious hedging strategies. Nevertheless, its participation in the Afghan campaign and in Iraqi reconstruction has set vital precedents for JSDF dispatch that mean that its security policy could potentially be drawn in radical new directions. For the first time, the JSDF has been dispatched during ongoing conflicts, and it now has a new mandate to use weapons not only to defend itself but also personnel under its responsibility, including refugees and US servicemen. Its geographical scope of operations, restricted for 50 years to East Asia, has rapidly expanded: in the space of three years, it has extended as far as the Middle East (see map see p. 13). Japan has acquired a new determination in its commitment to JSDF dispatch, its operations in Iraq derailed neither by the withdrawal of Spanish troops in 2004, nor by the traumatic kidnappings of Japanese citizens in Iraq in April, the killing of Japanese journalists in May, and the beheading of a Japanese hostage in October. In fact, public opinion has remained relatively supportive of GSDF dispatch despite these incidents.

The first radical development opened up for Japan by the 'war on terror' is an enhanced role in UN-centred multilateral operations through the option of collective security. As noted above, in devising the ATSML and LCSMHRA, Japanese policymakers have circumvented constitutional restrictions, with the result that Article 9 could be read as no longer providing a guide as to what ways Japan should seek to contribute to international security and how it should do so in terms of the restrictions on the use of force available. Instead Article 9 now merely provides a guide to the restrictions on the use of force, whereas the legitimisation for what Japan should seek to do to contribute to international security is now provided by the Preamble. This shift in constitutional interpretation has resulted in, whether deliberately or inadvertently, the same type of collective security option as first proposed by Ichiro Ozawa in the aftermath of the Gulf War. If Japan were to exercise this latent security option in the future, it would be able to participate in all forms of UN-sanctioned security activities, including peace enforcement, both in conjunction with and separate from the US. Japan's collective security option could enable expanded US–Japan cooperation in a new range of UN mandated missions, such as that of the Gulf War. However, it could also allow Japan, based on UN resolutions, to remove its military capabilities from the context and control of the bilateral alliance and place these under the control of the UNSC. In certain instances, where there is no UN mandate to act, US–Japan cooperation outside the ambit of the UNSC could then actually be prevented. Thus, Japan is faced with a military role that is potentially greater than that decreed by the US–Japan alliance, and could even function as an alternative. It is for precisely this reason, however, that Japan is unlikely to adopt collective security as an overt basis for its future security policy. Japan's collective security option could check bilateral cooperation with the US, engendering US concerns about the utility of the alliance and raising the risks of abandonment for Japan.

Japan is more likely to pursue a second radical development in its security policy heralded by the 'war on terror', drawing on the precedents of constitutional interpretation and functional cooperation that the war has set. JSDF deployment is likely to realise an expanded multilateral role for Japan along the lines of missions in Afghanistan and Iraq, but this is likely to be within the context of US-centred ad hoc multilateral 'coalitions of the willing' with a limited veneer of UN legitimisation, rather than within more UN-centred multilateral frameworks that might create an alternative space for Japan as a security actor. Japan has become accustomed to the practices of multilateral interaction under US tutelage and among US partners, whether it is refuelling UK ships, transporting Thai army equipment, or receiving Dutch army protection. Hence, Japan may have access to a multilateral space for security interaction, but it is ultimately a US-created space that has to date served primarily US-directed missions and, arguably, interests as well. Japan is not learning the real substance of multilateralism within its own East Asia region, or in developing existing multilateral frameworks in the region, or as a way to balance its heavy bilateral dependence on the US, as other 'normal' developed states have often sought to do.

The US-led PSI is another portent of this type of multilateral role for Japan. Japan is envisaged as the main sponsor of the PSI in East Asia, and in September 2003, JCG ships participated alongside US and Australian navy vessels off the coast of Australia in practise drills to intercept merchant vessels carrying WMD. The PSI is set to include other East Asian partners, South Korea and Singapore. Japan's efforts to include China were rebuffed by the US. Japan at first pulled out of the sponsorship of PSI drills close off its territorial waters scheduled for May 2004, concerned as it was by North Korea's reaction and how this may have affected ongoing Japanese diplomatic efforts over the abductions cases, and by the ASEAN states' lack of support in general for the PSI.[21] However, following Koizumi's visit to Pyongyang that year, Japan resumed its sponsorship of PSI drills for 26 October 2004. MSDF aircraft and the JCG, alongside vessels from the US, Australia and France, conducted drills in Sagami Bay, south of Tokyo, for the halting and inspection of ships suspected of carrying WMD. Japan's role as a key member of PSI stands as another example of US-led coalition-style multilateralism that only draws in certain members of East Asia and is weakly legitimised in international law.

In turn, Japan's multilateral activity may only serve to strengthen the bilateral alliance with the US. The provisions of the ATSML will set precedents that are likely to be applied to the context of the security treaty in East Asia. Japan, despite its attempts to construct constitutional firewalls between its support for the US in the context of the 'war on terror' and the US–Japan security treaty in East Asia, will find it politically difficult to hold this line in the event of a regional contingency. The US is likely to ask why Japan can provide certain types of support in Afghanistan and Iraq, but not in its own region, engendering alliance pressures to apply the same rules for

JSDF dispatch in these contexts to East Asia. Once again, then, multilateral activity by Japan may ultimately serve to supplement the strength of bilateral security relations.

Conclusion

Since the end of the Cold War, Japan has been undertaking greater regional and global security activity through the exploration of a variety of bilateral and multilateral frameworks. These include bilateral and multilateral security dialogue and anti-piracy operations in East Asia; UN PKO; and participation in the 'war on terror' in multinational coalitions. Japan's multilateral role has opened up potential avenues for cooperation with neighbouring states and those further afield. However, Japan's multilateralism should in no way be regarded as a major divergence from its overall post-war security trajectory in the sense that it is moving away from closer cooperation with the US. Instead, Japan has envisaged and utilised multi-lateralism, whether ARF security dialogue or dispatch to the Afghan campaign and Iraq, as subordinate and supplementary to the exigencies of bilateralism, and as means to accelerate its existing security trajectory along the path of strengthening the US–Japan alliance. Hence, Japan is reluctant to commit itself to expanded UN PKO or a collective security option as forms of multilateral commitment because they may conflict with the bilateral basis of its security policy.

Japan's ascribing of a supplementary and subordinate role to multilateralism in its security policy is unlikely to change in the near future. It will continue to support multilateral regional security dialogue, which, even in its currently circumscribed form, will be an important contribution to regional stability. Japan will take on slightly expanded UN PKO. Moreover, since mid-2003, Japanese policymakers, most notably Koizumi, Ishiba and Fukushiro Nukuga, LDP Chairman of PARC, have begun to discuss proposals for a permanent JSDF force available for international peace cooperation, or, as suggested by the LDP's DPSS and currently under investigation by a Cabinet Secretariat team, a single law that will obviate the need to pass individual laws for JSDF deployment on logistical support and humanitarian missions such as in Afghanistan and Iraq.[22] This may provide Japan with more flexible means for JSDF dispatch, but the essential purpose of this multilateral force in serving core bilateral alliance aims probably will not change. For instance, a JSDF international peace cooperation force may be available to the UN, but it will be available also for dispatch for multilateral 'coalitions of the willing'. Given the importance of US–Japan alliance ties, the prevailing political situation of strong domestic elite support for bilateralism and Japan's increased confidence in cooperation with the US gained from the operations in Afghanistan and Iraq, dispatch for multilateral 'coalitions of the willing' will likely be the JSDF's prime purpose under such a law. Likewise, Japan has now re-legitimised JSDF deployment to Iraq on the basis of UN Resolution 1546 and joined the re-branded US-led multinational force in a continued non-combat role (now probably in December 2004 to be extended beyond the initial one year period by at least six months), this time, with an even thicker veneer of UN multilateral legitimisation. Nevertheless, Japan's primary use of this mission – to undergird confidence in the bilateral US–Japan alliance – will not change.

Conclusion

So what is the overall trajectory of Japan's security policy over the past decade and in the immediate future? Is Japan re-emerging as a 'normal' or even great military power in regional and global military affairs? Is it seeking to chart a future security course that involves becoming an even stronger US ally, a bigger player in multilateral frameworks, or a more assertive independent military actor? What are the overall implications for regional and global security of Japan's security trajectory? These are the fundamental questions that this paper attempts to address.

Japan locks itself into the US–Japan alliance

Japan's past security trajectory is encapsulated by the Yoshida doctrine and its various adjustments during the Cold War period. Under this doctrine, Japan adopted a low-profile military posture and turned its energies and attention to economic reconstruction, with the eventual aim over the longer term of recovering great power economic status, and even great power military status. Japan's expedient choice of means to achieve these ends was alignment with the US and the concomitant strategic bargain represented the US–Japan security treaty: Japan would accept military protection from the US in return for the provision of bases. Japan's reliance on the US military guarantee, however, was tempered by the belief that it should avoid the alliance dilemmas of abandonment and, especially, entrapment as a consequence of US regional and global military strategy. In accordance with the Yoshida doctrine, Japan's watchword was that it would ultimately seek cooperation with, not dependence upon, the US.[1]

As the Cold War progressed, and as alignment gave way to a form of alliance, Japan–US security cooperation came to be characterised by an essential complementarity, but also by asymmetry and separation of capabilities and roles, with the US acting as the offensive 'sword' and Japan as the defensive 'shield'. Japan's security role in East Asia remained indirect, via the bilateral framework of the US–Japan alliance; it was geographically limited; it eschewed multilateralism, both in the form of collective self-defence and cooperative security dialogue; and its pace of expansion remained incremental. Above all, Japan's choice of this security policy was driven by continued wariness of the integration of its capabilities into US strategy for fear of entrapment. Japan's cautious, low-profile security policy was further reinforced by the domestic policy-making system, including strong constitutional prohibitions, rigid civilian control over the military, weak executive power and a political system divided over security issues.

Japan's security in the post-Cold War period has in many ways continued to follow the path-dependent approach of the Yoshida Doctrine, but has also begun to assume a more assertive military posture. As a result, it has accelerated along the trajectory of enhanced cooperation with the US while increasingly neglecting to observe many of the doctrine's key principles. Japan's evolving security policy has been occasioned by the changing strategic environment and a series of key security crises in the East Asia region and beyond. The Gulf War, the North Korean nuclear crises, the Taiwan crisis, the rise of China, 11 September and the 'war on terror' have all convinced Japan that the status quo in its security policy and the strategic bargain with the US are no longer tenable in their current form. Japan is now in the throes of a fundamental debate on its future security trajectory and how it can achieve the elusive mantle of a 'normal' state. Japan's most influential policymakers in the Kantei, MOFA, JDA, JSDF, LDP (all undergoing significant generational changes), along with the opposition DPJ (whose security stance is converging towards that of the LDP), are increasingly shifting to a position that the route to 'normality' lies in the strengthening of US–Japan alliance cooperation, out-of-area JSDF dispatch and the gradual abandonment of previous constitutional constraints, including, most notably, the exercise of the right of collective self-defence. Japan's anti-militaristic public is increasingly convinced by such arguments and shows less resistance than it might have to the potential expansion of Japan's military role.

Japan's shift in security policy has been reinforced and facilitated by a newly proactive policymaking system. The military establishment, in the shape of the JDA and JSDF, has risen to a more equal and 'normal' status vis-à-vis MOFA in the devising of security policy. Meanwhile, the prime minister's ability to conduct top-down and decisive leadership over security policy has been made possible not only by the phenomenal popularity of Koizumi, but more importantly, by the restructuring of the Kantei's coordinating power. The domestic party-political deadlock over security policy has been broken by the demise of the left-wing SDPJ and emergence of the DPJ, giving Japan two main political parties dedicated to a more proactive security stance. All of these actors have reached a rough consensus that Japan's security destiny continues to lie predominantly with the US–Japan alliance, although they differ over how far Japan should pursue alternative multilateral military options as well.

Japan's decisions about the development of its national security doctrines and capabilities reflect this new proactive stance. The revised NDPO of 1995 served to further embed the bilateral alliance at the heart of national security doctrine. The second revised NDPO, scheduled for 2004–05, should direct Japan towards a more flexible and mobile JSDF force structure suited to a range of new operations in support of the US and UN. Japanese policymakers have been involved in intensive rounds of passing emergency legislation in the Diet since 2002, to better prepare Japan for domestic security crises and to facilitate the operation of US forces in Japan.

Japan has been constrained to some extent in its acquisition of a more flexible and multi-operational JSDF force structure by limited defence budgets. Nevertheless, it is continuing a qualitative build-up of JSDF capabilities, including, most notably: the MSDF's NTWD BMD assets, amphibious capabilities and the rehearsal of aircraft carrier technologies; and the ASDF's PAC-3 BMD system, F-2 fighters and in-flight refuelling. In sum, these represent new JSDF power-projection capabilities for a range of missions, such as UN PKO, but that can also be used to support US-led expeditionary campaigns, as in Afghanistan and Iraq. Japan has complemented this hardware with the introduction of RMA-type BMC4I systems, and a new JSO for streamlined operational decision-making. Japan sees this as essential to maintaining an edge over regional rivals and to enable improved interoperability with the US. Japan has further acquired and integrated new intelligence capabilities in the form of the JDA's JDIH and the spy satellite programme. The acquisition of these intelligence capabilities, although triggered by concerns about over-dependence on the US, should not be seen as marking any weakening of the alliance, as they are essentially designed to give Japan a degree of greater autonomy within the existing framework of the alliance.

Japan has hinted at challenging a number of its post-war constitutional prohibitions. Contrary to foreign and domestic media speculation, Japan has not yet adopted a pre-emptive strike doctrine, but does stress, in more forceful fashion, its right to strike against hostile missile sites if Japan is sufficiently threatened. Discussion of a nuclear option has largely ceased to be a taboo, but Japan is highly unlikely to follow this path as a long as the US–Japan alliance remains intact, given the strategic, technological and financial costs. However, Japan is likely to end its ban on the export of arms to pave the way for greater US–Japan technological cooperation and to save its beleaguered defence production base. In the end, though, Japan is likely to become ever more dependent on black-boxed US military technology.

Japan's national military doctrines and capabilities indicate an overall drive to expand the possibilities of cooperation with the US. This is matched by Japanese and US bilateral moves to strengthen the alliance itself. Following the alliance shocks of the early 1990s, Japan and the US have rehabilitated their bilateral security relationship through the 1996–97 revision of the Defence Guidelines. The two countries have finally filled in the alliance's operability gaps left over from the Cold War period, shifted its focus from Article 5 to Article 6 of the security treaty, and upgraded its functions to respond to regional contingencies such as North Korea and Taiwan. Thus, Japan has sought to equalise the asymmetries of the alliance; however, throughout the period of revision, Japan retained its hedging options by using the concept of 'situational need' to obfuscate the geographical and functional scope of its support to the US. In this way, Japan has still been following the lessons of the Yoshida doctrine of cooperation with the US while avoiding overly close integration for risks of entrapment.

However, Japan's decision since December 2003 to acquire an off-the-shelf BMD system from the US represents a move to overturn key principles of the Yoshida doctrine. Japan–US security cooperation will be immeasurably enhanced, but the nature of BMD technologies mean that Japan will become inescapably dependent on the US and its risks of entrapment in regional contingencies will be accentuated. Japan will face an increased security dilemma vis-à-vis China. Japan's reliance on US BMD sensor technology will oblige it to further structure its security policy to accommodate the US; it will face calls for the deployment of its BMD system for defensive purposes in a range of contingencies; it will need to integrate its command-and-control and military forces far more with those of the US; and it will most probably need to end its ban on collective self defence – thereby creating an open-ended range of bilateral cooperation, including the most 'normal' role of all for an ally: fighting in combat alongside the US.

Japan's heightened cooperation and integration with US strategy in the bilateral context of the alliance is reinforced by its new activities in regional and global multilateral frameworks. Japan has played an important confidence-building role in regional multilateral security dialogues, such as the ARF; however, it regards these multilateral frameworks as necessarily subordinate and supplemental to the bilateral US–Japan alliance, rather than as alternative forms of building security cooperation. In certain cases, the functions of these multilateral fora are actually undercut by Japan's predominant bilateralism. Japan's participation in UN PKO has opened up an alternative multilateral and 'normal' security role for the JSDF. Nonetheless, this genuinely UN-centred multilateral role for Japan has been superseded since 11 September by participation in US-dominated multilateral 'coalitions of the willing'. Japan has thrown its policy-making energies into JSDF dispatch to support the Afghan campaign and Iraqi reconstruction. Japan has used differing degrees of UN legitimisation for dispatch, and hedged round its commitments by maintaining a non-combat role and limits on the type of capabilities devoted to these operations. The core purpose here was to expand the types of support that it can provide to its principal ally; the objectives of the international community have been a secondary consideration. Japan is thus learning to be multilateral, but it is a US-led, hegemonic form of multilateralism that chiefly serves to supplement the bilateral alliance relationship and to empower the US. Under it, Japan's risks of entrapment are enhanced, and the Yoshida doctrine is distorted.

In sum, then, Japan is once again becoming a great military power in East Asia and, increasingly, globally. However, the additional obvious conclusion is that Japan will fulfil this role within the confines of the US–Japan bilateral alliance. Japan's individual national capabilities, its alliance upgrading and even its multilateral activities are all directed towards strengthening bilateral cooperation with the US. Japan has not yet totally given itself to the cause of US regional and global military strategy; however, its hedging options for managing the bilateral security arrangements are clearly shrinking as alliance cooperation tightens apace. BMD will probably be the tipping point. Japan has continued to follow the Yoshida doctrine in the sense that it has revised its strategic bargain with the US, continued to seek cooperation and accomplished the goal of returning to the international scene as an economic and now military power. But Japan's increasing assumption of a less asymmetric role in the alliance has meant that, somewhat ironically, it is now becoming overly dependent on the US, to the position where it cannot extricate itself from the alliance. It is losing interest in pursuing alternative options such as multilateralism and risks entrapment in regional contingencies. In this way, Japan stands at the brink of abandoning many of the most vital elements of the Yoshida doctrine in its search for 'normal' status.

Is Japan's commitment to this trajectory and its locking-in to US strategy irrevocable? If the JSDF in Iraq were to suffer heavy casualties, so raising public ire against expanded security responsibilities, or if North Korea were to recede as an immediate threat and legitimisation for many alliance developments, Japan might yet reverse from this course and seek new hedging options. However, if the JSDF were to become involved in combat in Iraq, the prevailing political climate suggests that this would only strengthen the arguments of those calling for the removal of seemingly unrealistic restrictions on JSDF operations and the exercise of the right of collective self-defence, leading to even further enhancement of cooperation with the US. Moreover, even if North Korea were to stabilise, the more substantial and shared threat of China will continue to push forward US–Japan alliance cooperation.

Japan might also seek to pursue other non-military related, comprehensive security options to balance its increasing emphasis on military security and the alliance. Japan's articulation of a 'human security' policy and its utilisation of ODA will continue as important contributions to traditional military-generated security problems and non-traditional security problems generated by the fallout from globalisation. Japan has espoused a twin-track approach to Afghan and Iraqi reconstruction of peacekeeping and financial assistance, and takes state-building very seriously: hosting in Tokyo the International Conference on Reconstruction Assistance in 2002 and pledging US$500m in aid; and pledging US$5bn at the Madrid International Donors' Conference on the Reconstruction of Iraq.

But even if it is the case that Japan's use of economic power actually addresses more fully and effectively the range of extant security problems facing East Asia and the bulk of its citizenry – and this is where Japan should enjoy a comparative advantage in articulating security policy, given its traditions of comprehensive security – this is not likely to form the future focus of attention for Japanese policymakers.[2] Japan's devotion of policy energy and resources to human security, in comparison to that expended on the 'war on terror', remains minor. Moreover, Japan's capacity for the use of economic power, although still large, is currently shrinking as its ODA budget is progressively cut. Japan lost its position as the number one ODA donor in the world to the US in 2001, and its overall ODA budget has been cut by around 30% in the last seven years.[3] Japan may get greater 'bang for its buck' as it reorients a smaller ODA budget to less – and fewer – infrastructure-focused projects and concentrates on smaller-scale social and economic post-conflict reconstruction, but the impression is still of a shift in Japan's comprehensive security policy away from economic and towards military means.

Japan and the regional security order: reinforcing US hegemony

If all indicators point to Japan concentrating upon an expanding military role enmeshed within the framework of the US–Japan alliance, then what are the implications for regional and global security? It is now possible to envisage a highly interoperable US–Japan military alliance machine, with even stronger mutually reinforcing 'sword' and 'shield' functions, capable of perpetuating US military dominance over the region. The impact on future East Asian security will be profound.

The tightening of US–Japan security cooperation means that there is unlikely to be any return to a system of bipolarity or tripolarity in East Asia.[4] China, despite its phenomenal economic growth and the continued upgrading of its military, is highly unlikely to be able to rise to the position of a 'counter pole' to the combined strength of the US and a remilitarising Japan. Japan's continued close attachment to the US in security terms, despite its economic gravitation towards China, means that it is improbable that Japan would seek to form a third pole in regional security. Moreover, its continued subordinate and dependent position on the US in the bilateral alliance rules out a US–Japan joint partnership, or 'bigemony', in managing security affairs in the region, as 'Japan handlers' in the US would like to argue.[5]

Regional hopes for a system based on multipolarity or some form of multilateralism are also likely to be frustrated by the strengthening of the US–Japan alliance.[6] A multilateral concert of powers approach is unlikely, given that Japan and the US, as the region's two most important military powers, work far more closely with each other than with any of the other states, creating a fundamental imbalance of power in their favour in the region.[7] Moreover, the ARF and other regional institutions are not yet at a stage at which norms of cooperation are so well-established that the use of force to settle inter-state conflicts is unthinkable, which means that a genuine security community is still some way off.[8] Indeed, this paper has argued that the US–Japan alliance is inimical to the growth of even cooperative security dialogue as the basis for such a security community.

Instead, the only type of truly functioning security multilateral frameworks that are compatible with the US–Japan alliance are US-directed 'coalitions of the willing'. The real impact of a strengthened alliance is not to create a platform for East Asian states to explore additional or alternative frameworks for security, but simply to reaffirm the US-dominated hegemonic framework of security in the region.[9] Many smaller states in the region may be content with this framework, given its record of generating inter-state security for those states aligned with the US, and its control over Japan's military build-up and potential as a 'loose cannon' in the region. However, China may have difficulties coexisting with this form of US hegemony, which threatens to constrain its great-power ambitions while further facilitating the expansion of Japanese military power. In the wake of 11 September, China has temporarily reined in its criticisms of the strengthening Japan–US alliance and concentrated on building economic ties with both states. However, China may soon return to rail against the strengthened US–Japan alliance, with obvious destabilising consequences for regional security. This would raise tough questions for Japan about its own security trajectory and how far it will side with the US against its neighbour. Nevertheless, Japan's near-irreversible dependence on the US, and its conviction that it is better to be entrapped than abandoned by its US ally, may mean that it is forced to fight alongside the US in any future conflict and even one against China.

Japan's decision to lock itself into the US–Japan alliance will have wider effects on global security. Japanese support for the Afghan campaign and Iraq has shown that the US–Japan alliance is no longer just an East Asian or Asia-Pacific alliance, but one that functions to reinforce the US's global military reach. Japan is crucial to US global military hegemony not only in the provision of key bases for the projection of military power from the Asia–Pacific to the Middle East, but also as a provider of 'boots on the ground' for military coalitions. Finally, Japanese devotion to the alliance will affect global security by adding one more large military player to the mix, while lessening Japan's interest in making a difference via the use of economic power. As a result of this trade-off, and Japan's final abandonment of its position as an exemplar of non-military approaches to security, the world as a whole may be poorer.

Notes

Chapter 1

1 Richard J. Samuels, *Machiavelli's Children: Leaders and Their Legacies in Italy and Japan* (Ithaca, NY: Cornell University Press, 2003), p. 207; John Welfield, *An Empire in Eclipse: Japan in the Postwar American Alliance System* (1998, London, Athlone Press), p. 46.
2 Hugo Dobson, *Japan and United Nations Peacekeeping. New Pressures and New Responses* (London: Routledge, 2003), pp. 49–57.
3 Peter J. Katzenstein and Nobuo Okawara, 'Japan's national security: structures, norms, and policies', *International Security*, vol. 17, no. 4, 1992 p. 92.
4 Kenji Hayao, *The Japanese Prime Minister and Public Policy* (Pittsburgh, PA: University of Pittsburgh Press, 1993), pp. 182–83.
5 Eiichi Katahara, 'Japan: from containment to normalization', in Muthiah Alagappa (ed.), *Coercion and Governance: The Declining Political Role of the Military in Asia* (Stanford, CA: Stanford University Press, 2001), p. 77; Kent E. Calder, 'The institutions of Japanese foreign policy', in Richard L. Grant (ed.) *The Process of Japanese Foreign Policy: Focus on Asia* (London: The Royal Institute of International Affairs, 1997), pp. 13–14.
6 Kent Calder, *Crisis and Compensation: Public Policy and Political Stability in Japan* (Princeton, NJ: Princeton University Press, 1988), pp. 437–38.
7 Glenn D. Hook, *Militarization and Demilitarization in Contemporary Japan* (London: Routledge, 1996), pp. 129–58.
8 Ibid., pp. 100–126; Anthony DiFilippo, *The Challenges of the US-Japan Military Arrangement: Competing Security Transitions in a Changing International Environment* (Armonk, NY: M. E. Sharpe, 2002), pp. 144–57.
9 J. A. A. Stockwin, 'Dynamic and immobilist aspects of Japanese politics', in J. A. A. Stockwin, Alan Rix, Aurelia George, James Horne, Daichi Ito and Martin Collick, *Dynamic and Immobilist Politics in Japan* (London: Macmillan, 1988), pp. 1–21.

Chapter 2

1 Akihiko Tanaka, 'The domestic context: Japanese politics and UN peacekeeping', in Selig S. Harrison (ed.) *UN Peacekeeping: Japanese and American Perspectives* (Washington DC: Carnegie

Endowment for International Peace, 1995), p. 92.

2 On the North Korean nuclear crisis and the Taiwan Straits crisis and the impact on the US–Japan alliance, see Christopher W. Hughes, 'The North Korean nuclear crisis and Japanese security', *Survival*, vol. 38. no. 2, pp. 79–103; Thomas J. Christensen, 'China, the US–Japan Alliance, and the Security Dilemma in East Asia', *International Security*, vol. 23, no. 4, spring 1999, pp. 49–80; Eric Heginbotham and Richard J. Samuels, 'Mercantile realism and Japanese foreign policy', *International Security*, vol. 22, no. 4, pp. 171–203.

3 Reinhard Drifte, *Japan's Security Relations with China since 1989* (London: Routledge, 2003), pp. 51–52.

4 *Japan Times Online*, 15 May 2004, http://www.japantimes.co.jp/cgi bin/getarticle.pl5?nn20040515b6.htm.

5 Christopher W. Hughes, *Japan's Economic Power and Security: Japan and North Korea* (London: Routledge, 2003), p. 203.

6 Robert D. Eldridge, *Okinawa and US-Japan Relations in the 21st Century: Bilateral and Trilateral Approaches to a Sounder Okinawa Policy* (Tokyo: Research Institute for Peace and Security Occasional Paper, 2002), p. 10.

7 Christopher W. Hughes, 'Japan's Aum Shinrikyo, the changing nature of terrorism, and the post-Cold War security agenda', *Pacifica Review: Peace, Security and Global Change*, vol. 10, no. 1, February 1998, pp. 39–60.

8 Ichiro Ozawa, *Nihon Kaizo Keikaku* (Tokyo: Kodansha, 1993).

9 Akihiko Tanaka, 'The domestic context: Japanese politics and UN peacekeeping', in Harrison and Nishihara (eds.), *UN Peacekeeping*, p. 95; Mike M. Mochizuki, 'American and Japanese strategic debates: the need for a new synthesis', in Mike M. Mochizuki

(ed.) *Toward a True Alliance: Restructuring US-Japan Security Relations* (Washington DC: Brookings Institution Press, 1997), pp. 43–82; Michael J. Green, *Japan's Reluctant Realism: Foreign Policy Challenges in an Era of Uncertain Power* (New York: Palgrave, 2001), p. 197; Tomohito Shinoda, 'Ozawa Ichiro as an actor in foreign policy-making', *Japan Forum*, vol. 16, no. 1, 2004, p. 47.

10 Glenn D. Hook and Gavan McCormack, *Japan's Contest Constitution: Documents and Analysis* (London: Routledge, 2001), pp. 165–168.

11 Mike M. Mochizuki, 'Japan's search for strategy', *International Security*, vol. 8, no. 3, winter 1983/84, pp. 166–168; Mike M. Mochizuki, 'American and Japanese strategic debates: the need for a new synthesis', in Mike M. Mochizuki (ed.), *Toward a True Alliance: Restructuring US-Japan Security Relations* , p. 63.

12 Mochizuki, 'American and Japanese strategic debates: the need for a new synthesis', pp. 59–62.

13 Defence Policy Studies Subcommittee, National Defence Division, Policy Research Council, Liberal Democratic Party, *Recommendations on Japan's New Defence Policy: Toward a Safer and More Secure Japan in the World*, 30 March 2003, http://www.jimin.jp/jimin/main/seisaku.html, p. 4.

14 Ibid., p. 7.

15 Ibid., pp. 12–13.

16 Eugene A. Matthews, 'Japan's new nationalism', *Foreign Affairs*, vol. 82, no. 6, November/December 2003, pp. 74–90.

17 J. A. A. Stockwin, *Governing Japan: Divided Politics in a Major Economy* (Oxford: Blackwell Publishers, 1999), pp. 76–77.

18 Patrick Köllner, 'Factionalism in Japanese political parties revisit-

ed, or how do factions in the LDP and DPJ differ?', *Japan Forum*, vol. 16, no. 1, 2004, pp. 96–100.

19 Reiji Yoshida, 'Maehara Brokers Consensus, Compromise. DJP security advocate bridges internal, LDP gaps', *Japan Times Online*, 19 June 2003, http://www.japantimes.co.jp/cgi-bin/getarticle.pl5?nn20030619b1.htm.

20 Yoichi Funabashi, *Nihon no Taigai Koso: Resisengo no Bijiyon o Kaku* (Tokyo: Iwanami Shinsho, 1995), pp. 197–201; Yoichi Funabashi, 'Japan and the New World Order', *Foreign Affairs*, vol. 70, no. 5, 1991/1992, pp. 58–74.

21 Mochizuki, 'American and Japanese strategic debates: the need for a new synthesis', pp. 64–66.

22 Christopher W. Hughes, *Japan's Economic Power and Security: Japan and North Korea* (London: Routledge, 1999).

23 Green, *Japan's Reluctant Realism*, p. 69.

24 Asagumo Shimbunsha, *Boei Handobukku 2003* (Tokyo: Asagumo Shimbunsha, 2003), pp. 765, 814; *Yoron Chosa Heisei 15nen*, http://www8.cao.go.jp/survey/h14/h14-bouei/images/zu02.gif.

25 *Boei Handobukku 2003*, pp. 772, 821; *Yoron Chosa Heisei 15nen*.

26 *Boei Handobukku 2003*, pp. 769, 818; *Yoron Chosa Heisei 15nen*.

27 *Boei Handobukku 2003*, pp. 767–768.

28 Axel Berkofsky, *Corruption and Bribery in Japan's Ministry of Foreign Affairs: The Case of Suzuki Muneo*, JPRI Working Paper, no. 86, June 2002, http://www.jpri.org/publications/workingpapers/wp86.html.

29 Green, *Japan's Reluctant Realism*, p. 64.

30 Sabine Frühstück and Eyal Ben-Ari, '"Now we show it all!" Normalization and the management of violence in Japan's armed forces', *Journal of Japanese Studies*, vol. 28, no. 1, winter 2002, pp. 1–40.

31 Eiichi Katahara, 'Japan: from containment to normalization', p. 82.

32 Boeichohen, *Boei Hakusho 2002* (Tokyo: Zaimusho Insatsukyoku, 2002), p. 88; Boeichohen, *Boei Hakusho 2003* (Tokyo: Zaimush? Insatsukyoku, 2003), p. 90.

33 Richard J. Samuels, *Politics, Security, and Japan's Cabinet Legislation Bureau: Who Elected These Guys Anyway?*, JPRI Working Paper, no. 99, March 2004, pp. 8–10, http://www.jpri.org/publications/workingpapers/wp99.html.

34 *Taigai Kankei Tasuku Fosu, Niju Isseiki Nihon Gaiko no Kihon Senryaku – Arata na Jigai, Aratna Bijiyon, Arata na Gaiko*, 28 November 2002, http://www.kantei.go.jp/jp/kakugikettei/2002/1128tf.html; *Kokusai Heiwa Kyoryoku Kondankai, Kokusai Heiwa Kyoryoku Kondankai Hokokusho*, 18 December 2002, http://www.kantei.go.jp/jp/singi/kokusai/kettei/021218houkoku.html.

35 Tomohito Shinoda, 'Koizumi's top-down leadership in the anti-terrorism legislation: the impact of political institutional changes', *SAIS Review*, vol. 23, no. 1, winter–spring 2003, pp. 27–28.

36 'Haken e Kantei hashiru', *Asahi Shimbun*, 27 September 2001, p. 3; Shinoda Tomohito, 'Koizumi Shusho no ridashippu to anzen hosho seisaku katei', *Nihon Seiji Kenkyu*, vol. 1, no. 2, 2004, pp. 49–54.

37 'Seifu no anzen taisaku tesaguri', *Nihon Keizai Shimbun*, 10 February 2004, p. 2.

38 Research Commission on the Constitution, House of Representatives, Interim Report, November 2002, http://www.japanesepoliticians.com/search.cfm?fuseaction=linkdetail&category=Constitutional%20Revision.

39 '62% running for Upper House

support changing Constitution', *Japan Times Online*, 21 June 2004, http://www.japantimes.co.jp/cgi-bin/getarticle.pl5?nn20040621a1.htm.

Chapter 3

1. Yoichi Funabashi, *Alliance Adrift* (New York: Council on Foreign Relations Press, 1999), pp. 265–266.
2. Anzen Hosho to Boeiryoku ni Kansuru Kondankai, *Anzen Hosho to Boeiryoku ni Kansuru Hokokusho: Mirai e no Anzen Hosho, Boeiryoku Bijion*, October 2004, http://www.kantei.go.jp/jp/singi/ampobouei/dai13/13siryou.pdf.
3. 'Plans call for 7,000 new troops', *Asahi Shimbun*, 15 September 2004, http://www.asahi.com/english/politics/TKY200409150130.html.
4. Boeichohen, *Boei Hakusho 2004* (Tokyo: Zaimusho Insatsukyoku, 2004), pp. 325–329.
5. 'Kantei shudo irokoku', *Nihon Keizai Shimbun*, 21 April 2004, p. 2.
6. Boeichohen, *Boei Hakusho 2003* (Tokyo: Zaimusho Insatsukyoku, 2003), p. 158.
7. Shusho Kantei 'Yuji Hosei Kanren Horitsu', http://www.kantei.go.jp/jp/singi/hogohousei/houan/index.html; JDA, 'Yuji Hosei Kanren Horitsuan',http://www.jda.go.jp/j/library/law/yuji/index_a.htm.
8. Hartwig Hummel, 'Japan's military expenditures after the Cold War: the "realism" of the peace dividend', *Australian Journal of International Affairs*, vol. 50, no. 2, 1996, pp. 137–155.
9. Boeichohen, *Boei Hakusho 2003*, pp. 106, 340.
10. Ibid., p. 335.
11. Masako Ikegami-Andersson, 'Arms procurement decision making: Japan', in Ravinder Pal Singh, *Arms Procurement Decision Making. Volume I: China, India, Israel, Japan, South Korea and Thailand* (Oxford: Oxford University Press, 1998), pp. 46–147; Michael W. Chinworth, *Inside Japan's Defense: Technology, Economics and Strategy* (Washington DC: Brassey's, 1992), pp. 50–59.
12. 'GSDF inaugurates undercover antiterrorist squad', *Japan Times Online*, 30 March 2004, http://www.japantimes.co.jp/cgi-bin/getarticle.pl5?nn20040330a4.htm
13. 'Shin Chukibo no shuyo jigyo', *Securitarian*, March 2001, p. 13.
14. Boeichohen, *Boei Hakusho 2001* (Tokyo: Zaimusho Insatsukyoku, 2001), p. 99; MSDF, 'DDH kokeikan ni tsuite', http://www.jda.go.jp/JMSDF/topics/tyuubou/index322.html, Boeicho '2004 Seisaku Hyokasho (Goeikan 13,500-gata DDH)', http://www.jda.go.jp/j/info/hyouka/2003/jizen/san02.pdf.
15. 'Jikibo de tamokuteki sentoki sentei e, F2 chotatsu chushi de maetaoshi', *Yomiuri Shimbun*, 19 October 2004, http://yomiuri.co.jp/politics/news/200410191304.htm.
16. Boeichohen, *Boei Hakusho 2001*, p. 99.
17. Boeichohen, *Boei Hakusho 2003*, pp. 266–267.
18. Neil Renwick, 'Global economic change and cyber networks: East Asia's economic and security threats in perspective', in Christopher M. Dent (ed.) *Asia-Pacific and Security Cooperation: New Regional Agendas* (Basingstoke: Palgrave, 2004), pp. 210–211.
19. Boeichohen, *Boei Hakusho 2003*, pp. 305–306.
20. 'Admiral proposes SDF less run by civilians', *Japan Times Online*, 3 July 2004, http://www.japantimes.co.jp/cgibin/getarticle.pl5?nn20040703a1.htm.
21. 'ASDF to acquire JDAM bomb kits', *Yomiuri Shimbun*, 18 September 2003, p. 3; 'Agency

eyes longer reach', *Asahi Shimbun*, 27 July 2004, http://www.asahi.com/english/politics/TKY200407260187.html.

22 The GSDF's intelligence arm is the Nibetsu Investigation Bureau; the MSDF's is called Fleet Intelligence Command; and ASDF's is known as the Intelligence Division and Tactical Reconnaissance Group.

23 Yoichi Funabashi, *Alliance Adrift*, p. 115.

24 Desmond Ball and Euan Graham, *Japanese Airborne SIGINT Capabilities, Working Paper No. 353, Strategic and Defence Studies Centre* (Canberra: Australian National University Strategic and Defence Studies Centre, 2000), p. 17.

25 Isaku Okabe, 'Zenbo o bunseki. Nihon no joho shushu eisei', *Gunji Kenkyu*, vol. 35, no. 8, August 2003, pp. 71–73.

26 'Teisatsu eisei: kitai to kadai', *Asahi Shimbun*, 27 March 2003, p. 4.

27 Asagumo Shimbunsha, *Boei Handobukku 2003*, p. 557.

28 Boeichohen, *Boei Hakusho 1999*, pp. 91–92; Boeichohen, *Boei Hakusho 2003*, p. 90.

29 *156kai Shugiin Yosan Iinkai 4go*, 24 January 2003, p. 9.

30 Reinhard Drifte, *Arms Production in Japan: The Military Applications of Civilian Technology* (Boulder, CO and London: Westview Press, 1986), pp. 74–78.

31 Michael J. Green, *Arming Japan: Defence Production, Alliance Politics, and the Postwar Search for Autonomy* (New York: Columbia University Press, 1995), pp. 7–30; Chinworth, Inside Japan's Defence: pp. 38–39.

32 Tim Huxley and Susan Willett, *Arming East Asia*, Adelphi Paper 329 (Oxford: Oxford University Press for the IISS, 1999), p. 47; Richard J. Samuels, *Rich Nation, Strong Army: National Security and the Technological Transformation of Japan* (Ithaca, NY: Cornell University Press, 1994), pp. 26–31.

33 Arthur Alexander, *Of Tanks and Toyota: An Assessment of Japan's Defence Industry*, A Rand Note (Santa Monica, CA: RAND, 1993), pp. 52–53.

34 Shinzo Abe, 'Kaiken de kosenken mo mitomeru beki', *AERA*, 5 August 2004, p. 17.

35 Anzen Hosho to Boeiryokyu ni Kansuru Kondankai, 'Anzen Hosho to Boeiryokyu ni Kansuru Kondankai ni Okeru Kore Made no Giron to Gaiyo', http://www.kantei.go.jp/jp/singi/ampobouei/dai7/7siryou1.pdf.

36 Yuri Kase, 'The costs and benefits of Japan's nuclearization; an insight into the 1968/1970 Internal Report', *The Nonproliferation Review*, vol. 8, no. 2, summer 2001, pp. 55–68; Katsuhisa Furukawa, 'Nuclear option, arms control, an extended deterrence; in search of a new framework for Japan's nuclear policy', in Benjamin L. Self and Jeffrey W. Thompson (eds.) *Japan's Nuclear Option: Security, Politics and Policy in the 21st Century* (Washington DC: Henry L. Stimson Center, 2003), pp. 104–105

37 Eiichi Katahara, 'Japan's plutonium policy: consequences for non-proliferation', *The Nonproliferation Review*, vol. 5, no. 1, fall 1997, p. 59.

38 'Japan can be a nuclear power: Ozawa', *Japan Times Online*, 7 April 2002, http://www.japantimes.co.jp/cgi-bin/getarticle.pl5?nn20020407a1.htm.

39 Furukawa, 'Nuclear option, arms control, an extended deterrence', pp. 107.

40 'Nonnuclear policy to stay as is: Koizumi', *Japan Times Online*, 13 June 2002, http://www.japantimes.co.jp/cgi-bin/getarticle.pl5?nn20020613a6.htm.

41 Jeffrey W. Thompson and Benjamin L. Self, 'Nuclear energy,

space launch vehicles and advanced technology: Japan's prospects for nuclear breakout', in Self and Thompson (eds.) *Japan's Nuclear Option*, pp. 162–166.

42 Matake Kamiya, 'Nuclear Japan: oxymoron or coming soon?', *The Washington Quarterly*, winter 2002–2003, pp. 69–71.

Chapter 4

1 Funabashi, *Alliance Adrift*, p. 265.
2 Tetsuo Maeda, *Zainichi Beigun Kichi no Shushi Kessan*, (Tokyo: Chikuma Shinsho, 2000), pp. 162–165.
3 'Yokota no taihan Guamu e', *Nihon Keizai Shimbun*, 3 August 2004, p. 3.
4 'Japan mulls next missile defense stage', *Japan Times Online*, 18 December 2002, http://www.japantimes.co.jp/cgi bin/getarticle.pl5?nn20021218a2.htm
5 'Fukuda plays down comment on missile shield', *Japan Times Online*, 19 December 2002, http://www.japantimes.co.jp/cgi bin/getarticle.pl5?nn20021219a7.htm.
6 'Kuchu haibi reza Beikoku to no Kyodo kenkyu mo Ishiba Chokan shisa', *Asahi Shimbun*, 12 May 2004, http://www.asahi.com/special/s ecurity/TKY200405120291.html.
7 David Fouse, 'Japan gets serious about missile defence', *Asia-Pacific Security Studies*, vol. 2, no. 4, June 2003, p. 3; Boeicho, '2003 seisaku hyokasho (jizen no jigyo hyoka)', http://www.jda.go.jp/j/info/hy ouka/2003/jizen/hon01.pdf.
8 Tetsuya Umemoto, 'Ballistic Missile Defence and the US-Japan alliance', in G. John Ikenberry and Takashi Inoguchi (eds.) *Reinventing the Alliance; US Japan Security Partnership in an Era of Change* (New York: Palgrave Macmillan, 2003), p. 188.
9 For similar types of scenarios of JSDF defensive power and expe-

ditionary warfare in support of the US, as put forward by a Pentagon insider dealing with Japan, see Torkel Patterson, 'Future roles and missions of Japan's Self Defence Forces', in Ralph A. Cossa (ed.) *Restructuring the US-Japan Alliance: Toward a More Equal Partnership* (Washington DC: CSIS, 1997), pp. 133,136.
10 'US wants access to SDF radar data', *Japan Times Online*, 6 April 2004, http://www.japantimes .co.jp/cgibin/getarticle.pl5?nn200 40406a1.htm
11 'US eyes tighter military ties', *Asahi Shimbun*, 7 June 2004, http://www.asahi.com/eng- lish/nation/TKY200406070087.ht ml.
12 'Dando misairu geigeki kyodo kunren: Nichibei rainen medo kaishi', *Nihon Keizai Shimbun*, 7 June 2004, p.1.
13 Naikaku Kanbochokan Danwa, http://www.kantei.go.jp/jp/tyok an/koizumi/2003/1219danwa.ht ml.
14 Gen Nakatani, 'Waga kuni dokuji de misairu Boei mezasu', *Sekai Shuho*, 7 August 2001, p. 7.
15 Institute for National Strategic Studies, *The United States and Japan: Advancing Toward a Mature Partnership*, *INSS Special Report* (Washington DC: National Defence University, 2000).

Chapter 5

1 Paul Midford, 'Japan's leadership role in East Asian security multi- lateralism: the Nakayama propos- al and the logic of reassurance', *The Pacific Review*, vol. 13, no. 3, 2003, p. 379.
2 Ministry of Foreign Affairs Japan, *Diplomatic Blue Book 2003* (Tokyo: Ministry of Foreign Affairs, 2003), p. 124; Kuniko Ashizawa, 'Japan's approach toward Asian regional security: from 'hub' and 'spoke' bilateralism to 'multi-tiered', *The Pacific Review*, vol. 16, no. 3, 2003,

pp. 363–365.

3 For full details of Japan's bilateral security dialogue and exchanges, see Boeichohen, *Boei Hakusho* 2003, p. 353; and Christopher W. Hughes, 'Japan's subregional security and defence linkages with ASEANs, South Korea and China in the 1990s', *The Pacific Review*, vol. 9, no. 2, 1996, pp. 229–250.

4 The venerated war dead include 14 class-A war criminals, most notably General Tojo Hideki, and visits by Japanese leaders to the shrine often arouse regional controversy. 'Yasukuni sentei koryu', *Asahi Shimbun*, 10 January 2004, p. 2.

5 Japanese Shipowners' Association, 'Kaizoku koi ni kan suru chosa kekka ni tsuite', www.jsanet.or.jp/d2-3.html.

6 'Japan to send boat, jet, to Southeast Asia to fight piracy', *Japan Times Online*, 17 July 2002, http://www.japantimes.co.jp/cgi bin/getarticle.pl5?nn20020717c3.h tm.

7 *Yomiuri Shimbun*, 4 February 1999.

8 Euan Graham, *The Security of Japan's Sea Lanes 1940-2003: 'A Matter of Life and Death?'* (Unpublished PhD thesis, Australian National University, 2003), pp. 261–262.

9 For the 'quasi' and 'virtual' alliance concepts, see Victor D. Cha, *Alignment Despite Antagonism: The US–Korea–Japan Security Triangle* (Stanford, CA: Stanford University Press, 2003, 1999); Ralph A. Cossa, 'Peace on the Peninsula: how to get there from here', in Ralph A. Cossa (ed.) *US–Korea–Japan Relations: Building a 'Virtual Alliance'* (Washington DC: CSIS, 1999), p. 196.

10 Christopher W. Hughes and Akiko Fukushima, 'Japan–US Security Relations: "Towards Bilateralism Plus"?', in Ellis S. Krauss and T. J. Pempel (eds.) *Beyond Bilateralism: US-Japan Relations in the New Asia-Pacific*

(Stanford, CA: Stanford University Press, 2003), p. 84; Dennis C. Blair and John T. Hanley Jr., 'From wheels to webs: reconstructing Asia-Pacific security arrangements', *The Washington Quarterly*, vol. 24, no. 1, pp. 7–17.

11 Hughes and Fukushima, 'Japan-US Security Relations: "Towards Bilateralism Plus"?', pp. 80–81.

12 JMSDF homepage, http://www.jda.go.jp/JMSDF/ne wpage/hakenkyouryoku/sienkat udou/index.html.

13 The official English translation is, 'The Special Measures Law Concerning Measures Taken by Japan in Support of the Activities of Foreign Countries Aiming to Achieve the Purposes of the Charter of the United Nations in Response to the Terrorist Attacks Which Took Place on 11 September 2001 in the United States of America as well as Concerning Humanitarian Measures Based on Relevant Resolutions of the United Nations'.

14 Press Conference by Prime Minister Junichiro Koizumi, 9 December 2003, http://www.kan-tei.go.jp/foreign/koizumis-peech/2003/12/09press_e.html.

15 'Rikuji hontai mikka ni shuppat-su', *Nihon Keizai Shimbun*, 27 January 2004, p. 1.

16 The GSDF in Iraq intends to rely for protection against insurgents on Dutch forces. However, if a situation of danger arises that the Dutch are unable to prevent, the GSDF is permitted to use weapons for the defence of its own members and others under its control, such as local workers carrying out Japanese-backed projects. The GSDF is only to use weapons in cases of justifiable self-defence or in emergency evacuations, and to avoid harming human life. In principle, GSDF members use their weapons only if given a direct order by a commanding officer. GSDF members

in potential conflict situations need to follow a three-stage procedure: first, they must issue a warning in Arabic for insurgents to stop or be shot at; if this is ignored, the next stage is to fire a warning shot; and then, thirdly, shots can be aimed directly at the insurgents. GSDF members have expressed concerns that this three-stage rules of engagement system could prove impractical and a hazard to their own safety in fast-moving conflict situations requiring more decisive reactions.

17 'ASDF owns up to airlifting armed US troops to Iraq', *Japan Times Online*, 9 April 2004, http://www.japantimes.co.jp/cgi bin/getarticle.pl5?nn20040409a7. htm.

18 For examples of such views, see William Breer, 'Japan's contribution to the Campaign against terrorism', *Japan Watch, Center for Strategic and International Studies*, 18 October 2001; John Miller, 'Japan cross the Rubicon', *Asia-Pacific Security Studies*, vol. 1, no. 1, January 2002; The Atlantic Council of the United States, The Mansfield Center for Pacific Affairs and The Research Institute for Peace and Security, *New Frontiers for US-Japan Security Relations, Policy Paper*, February 2002, p. 2.

19 'Boeicho meiso', *Nihon Keizai Shimbun*, 6 February 2004, p. 2.

20 'Fuan kurasu Jieitai', *Nihon Keizai Shimbun*, 29 May 2004, p. 2.

21 'Nihon shusai kunren sakiokuri', *Asahi Shimbun*, 29 March 2004, pp. 1, 2.

22 'SDF peacekeeping force eyed by Defense Agency', *Japan Times Online*, 16 July 2003, http://www.japantimes.co.jp/cgi bin/getarticle.pl5?nn20030716a1. htm 'LDP lawmaker calls for permanent JSF dispatch law', 7 May 2004, http://www.japantimes.co.jp/cgi bin/getarticle.pl5?nn20040507a3. htm; Defence Policy Studies Subcommittee, *Recommendations on Japan's New Defence Policy*, p. 9.

Conclusion

1 John Welfield, *An Empire in Eclipse: Japan in the Postwar American Alliance System*, p. 104.

2 Christopher Hughes, *Japan's Economic Power and Security*, pp. 211–212.

3 'Nihon no ODA gaku, Bei no rokuwari ni shukusho', *Nihon Keizai Shimbun*, 18 April 2004, p. 8.

4 For the bipolar thesis and Japan, see Robert S. Ross, 'The geography of peace: East Asia in the twenty first century', *International Security*, vol. 23, no. 4, Spring 1999, pp. 90–92.

5 Takashi Ingouchi, 'Four Japanese scenarios for the future', *International Affairs*, vol. 65, no. 1, Winter 1988–89, pp. 20–22

6 Aaron Friedberg, 'Ripe for rivalry: prospects for peace in a multipolar Asia', *International Security*, vol. 18, no. 3, winter 1993–94, pp. 5–33; Richard K. Betts, 'Wealth, power, and instability: East Asia and the United States after the Cold War', *International Security*, vol. 18, no. 3, winter 1993–94, pp. 34–77.

7 Amitav Acharya, 'A concert of Asia?', *Survival*, vol. 41, no. 3, autumn 1999, pp. 84–101.

8 Emanuel Adler and Michael Barnett, 'Security communities in theoretical perspective', in Emanuel Adler and Michael Barnett (eds.) *Security Communities* (Cambridge: Cambridge University Press, 1998), p. 3.

9 Michael Mastanduno, 'The US-Japan alliance and models of regional security order', in G. John Ikenberry and Takashi Inoguchi (eds.) *Reinventing the Alliance: US-Japan Security Partnership in an Era of Change* (New York: Palgrave Macmillan, 2003), p. 27.